ESSENTIALS OF THE FAITH

I0233416

Proceeds from the sale of this book go to missions

CITIPOINTE CHURCH
LINKED TOGETHER TO IMPACT THE WORLD

ESSENTIALS OF THE FAITH

Book 3:
RELATIONSHIP

Gary L. Taylor

Essentials of the Faith: Book 3: Relationship/ Gary L. Taylor
ISBN: 978-1-959952-02-2

DEDICATION

To Rickey Shields, my friend and fellow laborer at Citipointe Church, Wylie, Texas. When the Lord connected us together over 30 years ago, I received a great gift. Rick is the personification of love. His servant's heart and genuine love for people are beyond measure. He clearly fulfills the Great Commandments: He loves God with the totality of his being and loves others as himself. Actually, he goes further than that – he loves others as Christ loves and gives himself for them

Beloved, let us love one another, for love is of God; and everyone who loves is born of God and knows God. He who does not love does not know God, for God is love. In this the love of God was manifested toward us, that God has sent His only begotten Son into the world, that we might live through Him. In this is love, not that we loved God, but that He loved us and sent His Son to be the propitiation for our sins. Beloved, if God so loved us, we also ought to love one another
—1 John 4:7-11

CONTENTS

ACKNOWLEDGMENTS

I would like to acknowledge the help of Blair Williams, Bob Potts, and Derek Smith, for all their work in editing and proofing these books. It is a tedious work for which I am eternally grateful.

INTRODUCTION

God created man with divine intent to fulfill a divine purpose. Essentials of the Faith leads the reader on a path of discovering the essential truths of that divine intent. The six-book series creates a solid, systematic understanding of who we are in Christ and how to live out that divine purpose.

BOOK 1: FOUNDATIONS

The concept of the vital principle of life is explored. Its creation by God, loss by man, and restoration by grace are examined.

BOOK 2: COVENANTS

The restoration of divine intent is based upon our covenant relationship with God. God's covenants with man are probed, and their benefits, conditions, and costs are revealed.

BOOK 3: RELATIONSHIP

Love demands expression, and God is love. Discover how we were created as recipients of that expression. As recipients, we become carriers of that expression.

BOOK 4: BLESSINGS

Christ is the Anointed One, and we are His followers. Examine the truth that as Christians, we are disciples of the Anointing. As such, we are blessed and carry a blessing.

BOOK 5: FAITH

The Scriptures are clear that without faith, it is impossible to please God. Put your faith on solid ground as you learn the principles and power of faith.

BOOK 6: CHURCH LIFE

No Christian is an island. We are all part of the body of Christ, and that body has organization, power, and life. Discover how each part fits together to fulfill God's divine intent.

1

GOD IS LOVE

*God is something existent, his love had no beginning;
because He is eternal, His love can have no end; Because He
is infinite, it has no limit; because He is holy, it is the
quintessence of all spotless purity, because he is immense,
his love is an incomprehensibly vast, bottomless, shoreless
sea before which we kneel in joyful silence and from which
the loftiest of eloquence retreats confused and abashed*
—A. W. Tozer

The story of the Bible is the story of relationship. In actuality, it is the greatest love story ever told. This great love story opens with the words, "In the beginning, God." In the vast darkness of pre-creation, God stood there all alone. Long before the first grain of sand fell through the eternal hourglass, God stood there in timeless infinity -- completely alone. Outside of time and space, before time and space even existed; there stood God in His infinite loneness.

But that infinite loneness could not continue for long. God's very being demanded relationship. In His essential essence, "God is love" (1 John 4:16). Love is the foundational building block upon which every other element of God's character rests. The fulness of God is the fulness of love. However, love cannot dwell together with loneness for long. Love demands relationship and fellowship.

Relationship is the lifeblood of life itself. Without relationship, there is no purpose or meaning in life. Without relationship, there is only the loneness of existence. Life without relationship is lifeless. Without relationship, there is no recipient for love's expressions. God is love, and His very being cried out for relationship and the fellowship that relationship provided.

All that we know was birthed out of God's desire for relationship. When He created man in His own image, He birthed relationship. Let your thoughts go all the way back to the Garden of Eden: what an idyllic life Adam and Eve experienced. At the very beginning of life on earth, they only had two responsibilities: love God and love each other. The essence of all relationship is love, and the expression of that love in fellowship. Without love, there is no real relationship or fellowship.

WHAT IS LOVE

The Merriam--Webster Dictionary[1] defines love as "a strong affection for another person based on kinship or personal ties." According to this definition, we love other people for one of two reasons, or possibly both. We either love them because they are part of our bloodline (family relationship), or we love them because we have similar tastes and desires (fellowship). In a best-of-all scenario, they are part of our bloodline, and we enjoy similar things.

When we apply that definition to God and His greatest creation, it seems to fit. God has an intense affection for humans, for they are part of His family. In the creation sense, then, humans are God's children. He created them out of Himself. Not only did He create us out of Himself, He created us like Himself. He created humans as rulers of the physical realm having personal responsibilities and activities similar to His.

---

[1] "Love." Merriam-Webster.com Dictionary, Merriam-Webster, https://www.merriam-webster.com/dictionary/love. Accessed 7 Dec. 2022

Nelson's Bible Dictionary [2] adds another dimension in its definition of Biblical love. Nelson's defines this relational love as "the high esteem, which God has for His human children and the high regard, which they, in turn, should have for Him and other people." While this definition removes the implied selfishness of the dictionary definition, it comes across as somewhat emotionless and impersonal. Love suddenly feels sterile and detached. The concept of intense affection is replaced with high esteem. In his great passage on love, the apostle Paul once wrote, "And now abide faith, hope, love, these three; but the greatest of these is love" (1 Cor 13:13). The tone of that passage changes rather drastically if we say, "And now abide faith, hope, and high esteem, but the greatest of these is high esteem."

While all relationships should include high esteem or high regard, true relationships are rooted in a substance that is far greater than simple respect. Relationships are based on love, which is a deep, personal essence derived from our Creator. While it evokes both intense affection and high esteem, these responses are but symptoms of a force far greater than either.

GOD IS LOVE

In his first letter to the church, the Apostle of Love wrote, "We have known and believed the love that God has for us. God is love, and he who abides in love abides in God, and God in him" (I John 4:16). God is more than objectified high esteem or sentimental, intense emotion. In the very depths of His being, He is super-passionate concern, care, and affection. Love is not just an attribute of God; it is the very essence of His being. Love is not simply something that God possesses; He is love. Every cell of His existence is established in and sustained by love.

This love of which John speaks goes beyond qualities and characteristics. This love pervades God's very being; it is the very essence of His infinite existence. At the very core of His being,

[2] Nelson's Illustrated Bible Dictionary, Copyright © 1986 by Thomas Nelson Publishers. All rights reserved. Used by permission

God is self-giving affection that knows no bounds. He does not just possess self-giving affection; He is self-giving affection. By definition, the word "infinite" means to have no boundaries. His love and affection toward us have no boundaries and no limits. What a wonderful thing to be loved by the God of creation with a limitless love!

Love is that intense inner warmth that cannot be objectively defined. We may not be able to define it accurately, but we know it when we experience it. Who can accurately define the feelings enveloping a parent holding a newborn child? But every parent knows that feeling even though a full explanation cannot be given. When it comes to our fellowship with God, that warm, inner experience is magnified, and human language is inadequate in expressing the depths of its meaning.

We accept the truth that God dwells in the infinite. All His attributes are boundless. We understand that God is omniscient. His knowledge knows no limits. He comprehends everything. We understand that He is omnipresent. His presence is not restricted by the physical boundaries of time and space. We understand that God is omnipotent. His power knows no limits. These are attributes that God possesses in His infinitude. But God does not simply possess infinite love. God IS boundless, infinite love in His very being. The love of God knows no limits.

But if God is love, why is the world so chaotic? The idea that a loving Creator allows the destructive evils we experience in this world causes an intellectual conflict for many people. We often hear questions like, "If God loves us so much, why does He allow so many bad things to happen?" "If God loves us so much, why would He send anyone to hell?" or "I could never love a God that condemns anyone to hell." Those kinds of questions and statements ignore the truth that man's actions do not change God's love. This truth is graphically laid out in Peter's second letter to the church.

2 Peter 3:9 states, "The Lord is not slack concerning His promise, as some count slackness, but is longsuffering toward us, not willing that any should perish but that all should come to

repentance." I particularly like the way Eugene Peterson interprets this verse in The Message. "God isn't late with his promise as some measure lateness. He is restraining himself on account of you, holding back the End because he doesn't want anyone lost. He's giving everyone space and time to change." People miss the opportunity of eternal life by their own volition -- despite God's loving intentions and desires. God loves every person with His limitless love. But He esteems us far too highly to violate our free will. We have been given a choice – it is totally our discretion where we spend eternity. He loves us so much that He made provision for our salvation. However, the acceptance or rejection of that provision is a matter of one's own personal volition.

He intensely desires that none should perish and that all should come into His kingdom of love. But that desire will never overrule His high esteem for the free will He has bestowed upon mankind. In His lovingkindness, He does all that He can to draw men to repentance. How often do people "despise the riches of His goodness, forbearance, and longsuffering, not knowing that the goodness of God leads you to repentance?" (Rom 2:4). We tend to place the blame on God for our own choices and fail to acknowledge His loving desire for us.

While it is His desire that all should enjoy the abundant life found in Him, He will not force men to receive that life. God will never force anyone to love Him. He will never force anyone to accept the boundless life and love found in Him. Man has a choice between life and death, heaven or hell. As that choice is placed before man, God subtly whispers in the ear, "Choose life!" (Deut. 30:19). However, this is where the high esteem comes into play – He will encourage us to make the choice for life and love, but He will never force life and love upon us. He will not violate our free will. He will allow us to choose hell and death if that is our desire. His high esteem is part and parcel of His love for us and prohibits Him from violating our free will.

One of the more well-known Scriptures on love is John 15:13. In this passage, Jesus says, "Greater love has no one than this, than to lay down one's life for his friends." And yet, God's love is greater still. He not only laid down His life for His friends, He laid down his life for His enemies—even those who crucified Him were loved by Him. Most of us would not think twice about dying for our family or friends, but dying for our enemies is a whole different dynamic. If you are a soldier, it is expected that you would be willing to die for your country and fellow soldiers. But it would be a totally different expectation to suppose that one would die to rescue an enemy combatant. But Jesus did just that! He died for those who hated and despised Him, as well as for those who loved Him.

One cannot imagine a greater love than that which Jesus expressed as the soldiers nailed Him to the cross. He prayed, "Father, forgive them. They don't know what they are doing" (Luke 23:34 MESS). Most of us would have prayed a vengeful prayer: "Lord, write their name in bold letters. Do not ever forget this moment. There will be a payday, someday!" But that kind of thinking never even came to His mind because He is love personified. This truth goes beyond the fact that He had great love: He is great love. Because He is infinite Love, He died for His followers and enemies alike.

LOVE IS GIVING

At its core, the Bible is the greatest love story ever told. From beginning to end, it depicts the love of God and His desire for fellowship. Because it is the story of love, it is the story of giving. The opening act depicts God giving existence to the totality of the physical realm. He gave life where there was no life. But with humans, His expression of love reached new heights. He went far beyond simple physical life. Into man, He breathed His very life essence. With that act, He breathed love into man. No other part of creation has that God-love breathed into its essence.

Love did not exist in our realm until God breathed that life essence of love into man. The book of Genesis tells us that God created us in His image: "And the LORD God formed man of the

6

dust of the ground and breathed into his nostrils the breath of life; and man became a living being" (Gen 2:7). If we are created in His image and He is love, then He created us as imagers of love. This truth is manifested in the life and teaching of Jesus.

He taught that the greatest commandment is to love God with all our being. Without reservation, He clearly stated that entering into a love relationship with God is of utmost importance (Matt 22:37-40). He went on to say that the second most important is loving one another. He made it clear to His followers that love is the defining mark of His disciples. He says, "By this, they will know that you are My disciples. You reflect My image. They will know you by your love" (John 13:35, paraphrase).

God created the entire universe, all of creation, for man. He did not create the earth and then think, "I need someone to inhabit this new creation." Before there was a physical creation, there was love. Before there was light, there was love. Long before God spoke the words "Let there be," mankind was in His mind's eye. His love demanded expression, and He created man as the recipient of that expression. All of creation was established to create a habitat for this recipient of His love.

As the beneficiary of God's expressed love, man was given the exclusive gift of relationship: relationship with God Himself and with fellow humans. God's relationship with the animal kingdom is not the same as His relationship with man. In the same respect, animals do not relate to one another in the same way as humans. He gave man the gift of relationship, unlike anything He gave to any other part of creation. This gift of relationship provided the foundation for fellowship and opened the door for all other gifts.

Love, by its very nature, is giving. James states that "every good gift and every perfect gift is from above, and comes down from the Father of lights, with whom there is no variation or shadow of turning" (James 1:17). The love of God (His very essence) demands expression. It insists on being poured out. As a father and grandfather, I can attest to the fact that bestowing gifts upon one's children is one of life's greatest joys. It is an expression of love that every father enjoys. If this is true of a physical father, how much more is it true of the Heavenly Father? His love delights in giving good gifts to His children.

No verse in the Bible better describes God's giving nature than the most famous of all Scriptures – "For God so loved the world that He gave His only begotten Son, that whoever believes in Him should not perish but have everlasting life" (John 3:16). Millions of sermons have been preached on this passage. God so loved that He gave. The concept seems simple, and yet at the same time, it is hard to fully grasp. The very essence of love is expressed in giving. By its very nature, love demands giving to express that which is within. A love that is not allowed expression is a frustrated thing.

God's love is never frustrated, for it is released in His giving. He has given us everything we need "pertaining to life and godliness" (2 Peter 1:3). Even the faith required to attain salvation is a gift from God. "But God, who is rich in mercy, because of His great love with which He loved us, even when we were dead in trespasses, made us alive together with Christ (by grace you have been saved), and raised us up together, and made us sit together in the heavenly places in Christ Jesus, that in the ages to come He might show the exceeding riches of His grace in His kindness toward us in Christ Jesus. For by grace you have been saved through faith, and that not of yourselves; it is the gift of God, not of works, lest anyone should boast" (Eph 2:4-9).

To attain salvation and enter into God's eternal family, God simply requires that we believe in Him. But He is unwilling to leave us groping for that essential element of faith. He loves us so much that He gives us the necessary faith to believe in His love for us. Paul writes in Romans 12:3 that "God has dealt to each one a measure of faith."

Because religion is a man-made thing, it tends to be man-centered. Religion always places man's works as a contributor to his salvation. In truth, there is nothing we can ever do to alter God's love for us. Our attempts at making God love us are like trying to buy favor from a rich friend. What can you do for God that will impress Him? At what price could you buy His favor?

When my son was young, he had feelings for a girl in his class. She invited him to her birthday party. So, he wanted to buy a gift for her and purchased a little necklace. He was too young to drive, so we drove him to her home for the party. The difficulty of his situation became apparent as we arrived at her house. Her house was so large that it occupied an entire city block. The home had a massive entryway, multiple swimming pools, tennis courts, and basketball courts. If he was going to impress this girl, it was not going to be with his limited financial resources. That incident illustrates the absurdity of us thinking that we are somehow going to impress God; that we are doing to somehow sway Him with our good works and gifts. He has everything. He owns everything. He can do everything, and He already knows everything! What could you possibly give Him to earn His love?

God is not looking for us to give to Him – He simply wants us to receive from Him. He wants our humility. Our God does not ask of us but rather gives to us. God does not ask us to 'do" for Him. He wants us to get out of the way so that He can live through us. David explains this in Psalm 51: "For You do not desire sacrifice, or else I would give it; You do not delight in burnt offering. The sacrifices of God are a broken spirit, A broken and a contrite heart — These, O God, You will not despise" (Ps 51:16-17).

Every command He gives is accompanied with the resources to accomplish the task. This truth holds true even with the basics of salvation. Scripture says that you have been "saved by grace through faith" (Eph 2:8). But He realizes that you do not even have faith. After all, you "were dead in your trespasses and sins" (Eph 2:1 NASB). And dead people have no ability to believe. So, God gave you the faith that is required for salvation. He always gives you everything you need for the requirements He places on you. When He calls you to do something, He is preparing you for the plans He has for you. He will give you the skills and resources to complete every task and purpose He has for you. "For we are

God's workmanship, created in Christ Jesus to do good works, which God prepared in advance for us to do" (Eph 2:10 NIV). He only places one requirement upon us. He simply requires that we humbly submit to Him and receive from Him what is needed to fulfill the task at hand.

For instance, Jesus taught to "give to everyone who asks of you" (Luke 6:30). That command requires substantial resources to fulfill. But if that is His command, He will provide the necessary resources to satisfy the command. We must learn to simply trust His promise to be our supply. Notice the straightforward promise of Philippians 4:19. "God shall supply all your need according to His riches in glory by Christ Jesus." He promises to supply ALL our needs, including the abundance necessary to enable us to give to everyone who asks of us.

Many Christians have trouble trusting God in the area of finances. They tend to believe that finances are their responsibility. But God is our financial source. Our wealth does not come from our employer. It may come through your employer, but it comes from God. When it seems like financial resources are not available, we must put our trust in Him. He is wealthier than the wealthiest man alive! He owns the cattle on a thousand hills, and his streets are paved with pure gold. It is foolish to believe that we know more about our finances and resources than He!

God's blessings flow from His love and are given to us through His promises. Our faith in those promises aligns us with His Word. As we align ourselves with His word we receive those blessings. The only requirement placed upon us is to get in alignment with His word! Many Christians live in turmoil because they are in the wrong queue.

If you get in the wrong queue at the airport, you will be sorely disappointed when you reach your destination. Many Christians are standing in the queue of their own works rather than standing in the queue of God's grace. They tend to believe that their right-standing with God is based upon their own works. They are going to be sorely disappointed when they reach their destination and suddenly realize that "all our righteousnesses are like filthy rags" (Is 64:6).

UNCONDITIONAL, "FIRST LOVE"

In the Book of Revelation, John records Jesus' letters to the churches. In His letter to the Church at Ephesus, He reveals to them that they have lost their first love. We often interpret this verse to mean that they have lost the love for God that they had at the beginning. But I believe He is referring to the loss of the First Love. God loved us first, before any other loves came along. Even in our mother's womb, God knew us...and loved us. In fact, He loved us even before that! Paul tells us in Ephesians 1:4 that "just as He chose us in Him before the foundation of the world, that we should be holy and without blame before Him, in love." He loved us at creation! He loved us before creation. God did not wait until we loved Him – He was proactive in His love.

We hear a lot of talk today about male and female roles. Today's society says that women should be aggressive, independent, and proactive. They do not have to wait for the man to move. Such was not always the case. In older stories, you will most often discover that the plot involves the man pursuing the girl. Scripture tells us that the Church is called the bride of Christ (Eph 5:23). God pursues the Church, not vice versa. He pursued you long before you pursued Him. As a matter of fact, you would have never pursued Him had He not pursued you first. He was proactive and went after us; we never went after Him until He went after us.

According to 1 John 4:19, "We love Him because He first loved us." Whenever you think about how much you love God, understand that you only love God because He first loved you. I am always amazed at people talking about loving God for who He is; not for what He does. That is impossible! You love God because He loved you. Just as the Scripture says, we love God because He loved us. He meets our needs, and we receive from Him – beginning with our salvation and continuing through life itself.

When we first come to Jesus seeking salvation, we have mixed emotions about His death. If we are honest with ourselves, we would say, "I am sorry that you died on the cross, but I sure am glad that you did!" We rejoice over the fact that He died for us. We came in with a somewhat selfish motivation, and it has never changed. God designed it that way! In the pursuit of us, His love forced Him to pay our penalty for sin. It is this sacrificial act of love that draws men to Him. In Romans 2:4, Paul tells us that "the goodness of God leads you to repentance." It is His lovingkindness, His goodness, that draws us to Him and makes us love Him.

God's love for us is not a reciprocal love – it is an unconditional love. That is not to imply in any way that He does not desire our love. But He does not tell us that He will love us if we love Him or if we do certain things for Him. It is not about what we can do for God but about what He did and will do for us and through us. He always loved the loveless; the ones who had nothing to offer Him. The men Jesus picked to be disciples were definitely not at the top of the "love" list. Matthew was a tax collector, cheating people out of their money. Peter, Andrew, James, and John were all fishermen. He did not pick the elite! Perhaps He picked the ones who needed love the most.

It is imperative that we remember that God's love is no respecter of persons. His love and affection is not greater for certain people. He loves all of us to such a degree that He took all our sin in His body on the tree. The Scripture says that He died "for our sins, and not for ours only but also for the whole world" (1 John 2:2). That is unconditional love. Whether we love Him or not, He still loves us. This is not only applicable to the Church but to the entire world. He loved Anton LaVey as much as He did Billy Graham. Anton LaVey founded the Church of Satan and wrote the Satanic Bible. Yet, God loved Anton as much as He loved Billy Graham, one of the greatest evangelists of our time. His love for us is not determined by our reciprocal love or the absence thereof.

His love is unconditional and unmerited. We tend to think that if we do certain things for God, He will love us more. If it were a merited love, that would be true. But His love is not based upon our actions or sacrifice. There is no way we could ever be good enough to deserve God's love. The Bible tells us that we are all sinners who fall short of His love. His love for us is based upon the fact that He is love.

I am often asked, "Do you believe in the doctrine of once saved, always saved?" The answer to that question depends on your definition of "saved." The word "saved" means "delivered or made whole." I do not believe in "once delivered, always delivered." I think everyone gets what they want. If you want to play with those demons, you can play with them. If you want to live in bondage, you can live in bondage. However, if you are talking about a man being made whole (born again), then no, I do not believe he can lose his new birth. How can that which is born become unborn? How can a son become a non-son?

Once we are born into the Kingdom, we are in the Kingdom. There is no turning back! We may not enjoy the full benefits of the Kingdom, but we are still of the Kingdom. The prodigal (excessive) son was always the son. No action of his could ever change his sonship. He was the son of his father regardless of his actions. However, his choices prohibited him from fully enjoying the benefits of his sonship. People can walk away from the Lord, but God will not walk away from them. His love is unconditional.

We point our fingers and say, "They have walked away from God. They have backslidden." Have we not all walked away and backslidden in some ways or at some times? God's kingdom requires perfection, so it only takes one sin to "backslide." We say, "They have turned away from God." At what point have we not? We are all guilty of the measuring of sin by degrees. Sin is sin, and it all has a putrid stench. It just so happens that we do not think that our sin stinks as badly as everyone else's...but it does!

Once we understand that He loves us, whether or not we reciprocate His love, great security is produced in our heart.

Galatians 5:6 tells "faith is activated and energized and expressed and working through love" (AMP). The level of your faith rests upon the level of your understanding of God's love. How many times do we read that Jesus was moved with compassion and then performed a miracle? His love compelled Him to resolve the misery in others. He was a man of great faith because He was a man of great love. The greater your understanding of God's infinite love, the greater your faith. You will never do great works of faith until you understand great love.

Great works of faith are often equated with great boldness. But great works of faith are actually just great works of love. Suppose a woman ran into a burning house to rescue her infant daughter from the fire. Would you call her a bold and brave woman? No, you would call her "Mom." She loves that child and will gladly give her life for the child. You would not call her a courageous, bold woman. You would speak of her love for the child. If she were to simply stand in the yard and let the girl die, you would question her love, and wonder about her heart. Even if the situation were hopeless, you would likely have to restrain her. She loves that child. Bold actions like this come from a heart full of love, not from simple courage.

LOVE OVERCOMES

Love is the only thing that overcomes fear. We often think that fear is a faith issue. But in reality, fear is a love issue. The person who walks in fear fails to understand the love of God. The love of God provides protection and power to our life. The person who walks in love walks in the presence and protection of God. The Scripture does not establish faith as the opponent of fear. It tells us that perfect love casts out all fear. "There is no fear in love [dread does not exist], but full-grown (complete, perfect) love turns fear out of doors and expels every trace of terror!" (1 John 4:18 AMP). We overcome fear with perfect love.

14

Psalm 139 speaks of the fact that God is always with us. It is a wonderfully encouraging passage. But it is even more encouraging when we remember that God IS love. What an encouragement when we substitute the "Love of God" into David's psalm.

"If I ascend into heaven, the Love of God is there; if I make my bed in hell, behold, the Love of God is there. If I take the wings of the morning, and dwell in the uttermost parts of the sea, even there the Love of God shall lead me, and Love's right hand shall hold me. If I say, "Surely the darkness shall fall on me," even the night shall be light about me; indeed, the darkness shall not hide from the Love of God, but the night shines as the day; the darkness and the light are both alike to the Love of God. For the Love of God formed my inward parts; the Love of God covered me in my mother's womb. I will praise the Love of God, for I am fearfully and wonderfully made; marvelous are the works of the Love of God, and that my soul knows very well. My frame was not hidden from the Love of God, when I was made in secret, and skillfully wrought in the lowest parts of the earth. Your eyes saw my substance, being yet unformed. And in the book of the Love of God they all were written, the days fashioned for me, when as yet there were none of them. How precious also are the Love of God thoughts to me, O God! How great is the sum of them! If I should count them, they would be more in number than the sand; when I awake, I am still with the Love of God.

What a comforting thought! No matter your situation or location, the love of God is with you. Remember, God is love. Wherever His presence abides, His love abides. Once the reality of that truth settles into your heart, fear dissipates. Comfort and boldness replace the fear as you realize that you are loved by the Creator and in that love, you have full protection. In his love letter to the church, the apostle, John ,wrote, "There is no fear in love; but perfect love casts out fear, because fear involves torment. But he who fears has not been made perfect in love" (1 John 4:18).

The idea that perfect love removes fear was not something I grew up understanding. In fact, quite the opposite was true. Fear of somehow falling away from God was ingrained in me as a child. Our church would have revival meetings at least twice a year, and guest evangelists would be invited to preach. As the evangelist preached, it made me feel so bad that I felt I needed to do something. So, I just kept "rededicating" my life to God over and over again. Religion puts the fear in you that you are not pleasing to the Lord and that He may not let you into heaven.

Years ago, I was ministering to a young man who was wrestling with the security of his salvation. An evangelist had preached in his church and proclaimed that you were not really saved if you sinned after you received Christ as your savior. This young man started telling us about his need for salvation. As he talked, it was clear that he had experienced some real encounters with God in the past. But he kept saying that he needed to be baptized again. During our conversation, he revealed that he had already been baptized seven times. He had no security in his salvation because he had no confidence in God's unconditional love.

As we just noted, 1 John tells us that love does not involve torment. Hell is going to be torment not simply because of the fire and gnashing of teeth. The worst part of hell will be the fact that for the first time in man's existence, he will know what it is to be totally cut off from the love of God. No matter how depraved a man is currently, the love of God is still within him. He may not receive it or believe it, but that does not change the love of God.

If you visit a prison, you will find hardened criminals holding some of the mushiest love sentiments. A "Mom" tattoo on their burly arm or letters from family are often their most prized possessions. Regardless of how hard they appear – the love of God is still there, no matter how unrecognizable. However, on

16

Judgment Day, love will be cut off from those who have not accepted His love gift of salvation through Christ Jesus. They will experience a total lack of love for eternity.

But no one needs to experience this love loss. Over and over the Scripture pictures God's precious love for us. In Psalm 139, David prays: "How precious also are Your thoughts to me, O God! How great is the sum of them! If I should count them, they would be more in number than the sand; when I awake, I am still with You." The prophet Jeremiah defines those thoughts for us. He says, "For I know the thoughts that I think toward you, says the Lord, thoughts of peace and not of evil, to give you a future and a hope" (Jer 29:11). So David is actually saying: "How precious are your thoughts of peace and not evil towards me, O God! How great is the sum of that love. If I should count those thoughts of love, they would be more in number than the sand. When I awake, I am still with you and your thoughts provide a future and a hope in me."

These are God's thoughts for us - thoughts of a future and a hope. Yet, they are so numerous, we cannot count them. No wonder the apostle Paul exclaims, "eye has not seen nor ear heard, nor have entered the heart of man the good things which God has prepared for those who love Him" (1 Cor 2:9). The good things of God are too high for us to even count. Our feeble minds cannot calculate a number that large!

Not only does He love us unconditionally, but He demonstrated that love for us unconditionally. I believe one of the greatest verses in the Bible is Romans 5:8, which reads, "But God demonstrates His own love toward us, in that while we were still sinners, Christ died for us." Years ago, we were having problems with our connecting flight at the Kathmandu airport. A young man working for the airline was very helpful and hospitable. He took us upstairs to the executive offices. He served us tea and as we talked, he revealed the fact that he believed Christianity and Hinduism were basically the same. His thoughts were that the two were simply different paths to the same place.

Obviously, he could not have been more wrong. In his belief system, he must continually work to achieve his reward. His hope is that his good works will cause him to be reincarnated into a better form of life. He will live his life waiting on a determination that is outside of his control. He has no way of knowing if his actions will be enough to promote him to a higher level of existence or if he will return as a cockroach in his next life. But as believers in the Lord Jesus Christ, we have our nirvana every day. Our reward has already been purchased.

When this fact was explained to the young man, his eyes widened in amazement. He could hardly believe it. But the revelation slowly settled in. God loved him and accepted him into his family knowing who he was and what he had done. The truth is that our God loved us so much that He did not wait. He did not wait for us to come to the light. He reached into the darkness of our sinful soul and loved us. He did not tell us to become righteous so He could love us. He loved us in our sinful, despicably fallen state and made us righteous. He accepted us into His family even though there was nothing acceptable in us.

LOVE IS OUR DWELLING PLACE

Jesus said that love would be the identifying mark of His disciples. He says, "By this all will know that you are My disciples, if you have love for one another" (John 13:35). John makes it even more clear in 1 John 4:20 when he says, "If someone says, "I love God," and hates his brother, he is a liar; for he who does not love his brother whom he has seen, how can he love God whom he has not seen?" Judgement Day is going to be problematic for a lot of "believers" who fail to understand the importance of love.

Jesus says that the world will know that we are His disciples by our love. If God is love and we are His children, then love should be our defining characteristic as well. If we dwell in God, we are actually dwelling in love. In John 15, Jesus challenges us to abide in Him. He says that we are the branches, and He is the vine. When we abide in Him, we are resting in love—for Jesus is the physical personification of love. That is what John is addressing in 1 John 4:16 when he says, "And we have known and believed the love that God has for us. God is love, and he who abides in love abides in God, and God in him." You cannot abide in God and not abide in love, for God is love.

Again, John 15 tells us that Jesus is the vine, and we are the branches. If the branch stays securely attached to the vine, the life forces of the vine flow through the branch. These life forces cause the branch to produce the fruit of the vine. Jesus says that if we abide in Him, we will produce much fruit. He goes on to say that this fruit glorifies the Father. The branch receives no glory for the fruit. It is the fruit of the vine. The believer who abides in Christ takes no glory in the fruit, for the fruit is the fruit of the Spirit of Christ flowing through us.

The branch does not work to produce the fruit. It simply abides in the vine. The believer does not produce the fruit. The believer simply abides in Christ, and the fruit of the Spirit is produced. Galatians 6 lists the fruit of the Spirit, and love is the first fruit listed. We do not work to produce love. We abide in Christ and His love flows through us.

As we abide in Christ and experience God's presence in every detail of our life, we will live in love. As we live in love, we express that love to others. If you say that you love God, but you do not love others, you deceive yourself. This love is to be expressed to all people of all races and socio-economic classes. We are to love all people as Christ loves us. This even applies to those we might perceive as "peculiar people". There are some strangely odd people in our world, but God loves them as much as He loves you and me. My dad was a bit of an arm-chair philosopher. In jest, he would say, "Everyone who isn't like you and me is different." The sad truth is that many people judge others by that standard. Everyone that is not like them is not normal. This concept of "normal" is a totally subjective and fluid standard. But Jesus did not command us to love "normal" people. He told us to love "others" as we love ourselves.

19

THE PRE-EMINENCE OF LOVE

Because God is love, love is of foremost importance. In his letter to the church at Corinth, Paul penned what is often referred to as the "love chapter" or the "love hymn." In the last verse of the chapter, he says, "And now abide faith, hope, love, these three; but the greatest of these is love" (1 Cor 13:13). Love is pre-eminent. Before faith, there is love. Before hope, there is love. Before everything, there is love.

Jesus detailed this in His answer to the question about which is the greatest commandment. He tells us that the greatest commandment is to love God, and the second is to love others. If we abide in Christ, this will be as natural to us as it was to Jesus. When Paul lists the fruits of the Spirit, he lists love first when he states, "But the fruit of the Spirit is love, joy, peace, longsuffering, kindness, goodness, faithfulness, gentleness, self-control. Against such there is no law" (Gal 5:22-23). And in his letter to the church at Colossae, Paul tells them that above everything else they are to "put on love" (Col 3:14). Love is the bond of perfection; God is love, and by loving, we are putting on God.

Let us return to 1 Corinthians 13 and substitute the word "God" for "love" in verses 4-8:

GOD suffers long and is kind; GOD does not envy; GOD does not parade Himself, is not puffed up; does not behave rudely, does not seek HIS own, is not provoked, thinks no evil; does not rejoice in iniquity, but rejoices in the truth; bears all things, believes all things, hopes all things, endures all things. GOD never fails. But whether there are prophecies, they will fail; whether there are tongues, they will cease; whether there is knowledge, it will vanish away.

God is love, and if we are going to live in relationship with God, we must live in love. Possibly the most challenging part of living in love is learning to love the unlovely. It is easy to love the beautiful people. It is hard to love the unbeautiful people. God's desire is for us to love our neighbors as Christ loved them. This command to love our neighbor is a progressive command. The command is first given as simply, "Love your neighbor." Then, the command moves to a higher level when Jesus says, "Love your neighbor as yourself" (Mark 12:31). In the final climax, Jesus says, "Love your neighbor as I loved you" (John 13:34). This last command moved love out of the reach of performance! It is much easier for me to love them as I love myself. Loving others as God has loved me means loving them unconditionally, despite their failures and oddities. I cannot attain to this kind of love on my own. I must allow the love of God to permeate me and love others with the love of God that is within me.

Many wonderful "relevant" sermons have been preached on the subject of loving others. We are told that before you can love your neighbor, you must learn to love yourself. Yet, that is the opposite of what is written in the Scriptures. There is not a single place in Scripture where you are instructed to love yourself. In fact, Revelation 12:11 tells us that those who overcome do not love themselves, even to the point where they willingly give up their lives. I know that our modern, pop-psychology church world tells us that we must learn to love ourselves. But that simply is not true. We must learn to love God and let His love invade us in such a way that we are overflowing with love. All our self-image issues will disappear when we let the light of God's love shine through us. God's love must invade us fully – until we are possessed with love.

When we come to the realization that God loves us absolutely, it really does not matter what anyone else thinks. If God says, "You are important," and some little peanut says, "You are nothing," who cares what the peanut says? Years ago, we were in relationship with a keyboard player who had played professionally for many years. He gave my daughter, Charity (also a keyboardist), a compliment about her musical ability. His simple comment forever changed her feelings about playing. If the professional musician told her she was doing well and some non-musician complained about her piano playing, whose opinion carried the most weight? Do you think she cared what the non-musician thought? We have not learned to tune our ears to the voice of the Lord. When we learn to listen to Him, it will not matter what anyone else says. If the dean of the college says that you are an exceptional student, it does not matter what the janitor says. Unfortunately, we tend to listen to the janitors in our life.

Your steadfast love, O Lord, extends to the heavens,
your faithfulness to the clouds.
Psalm 36:5 ESV

2

TYPES OF LOVE

Love is a better teacher than duty."
—Albert Einstein

At the end of the Gospel of John, seven of the disciples are fishing on the Sea of Galilee. Even though they have seen the resurrected Lord, they are a little confused about their purpose and mission. With no clear direction, Peter decides to go back to fishing, and the others decide to go with him.

Even though four of the seven are professional fishermen, they had fished all night and caught nothing. As they return to base, Jesus is standing on the shore and calls out to them, "Children, did you catch any fish?"

They answer back, "No."

Jesus tells them, "Cast your net off the right side of the boat and you will catch some fish."

With nothing to lose, the disciples follow His suggestion. To their surprise, they catch such an abundance of fish that they cannot even get the net into the boat. They catch over one hundred fifty fish and actually have to drag the net to shore. When the disciples finally get the fish to shore, they discover Jesus has a fire of coals prepared. He tells them to bring some of the fish, and He prepares breakfast for them. Then, they share a final meal of fish and bread together.

After breakfast, Jesus initiates an insightful conversation with Peter. Jesus asks Peter, "Do you love me?" And Peter responds, "Yes, Lord, you know I love you." Then the question and answer are repeated two more times with slight variation. One must wonder about the significance of all this repetition. After receiving confirmation of Peter's love for Him, why did the Lord keep repeating the question?

THREE TYPES OF LOVE

To fully understand this conversation, it is important to remember that the New Testament was originally written in Greek; the language of the Roman Empire. In the Greek language, there are three basic words translated as "love." Understanding the differences in these three words is imperative to interpreting this discourse between Jesus and Peter. But more importantly, it is also essential to understanding all relationships.

An unselfish, unconditional, God-kind of love is the first and highest form of love. The Greek word *agape* is used to express this kind of love. The second word expressing the concept of love is *phileo*. This word represents a natural affection that one person has for another and is sometimes called brotherly love. The last word is the word *eros*, and it is an erotic, lustful love. We will discuss each of these in detail, beginning with the least and progressing to the highest.

Eros Love

Eros is love at its lowest denominator. It is questionable whether we should even call it love. It could easily be referred to as lust. This is the Greek word from which we get the English word erotic. It is a sensual love limited to relationships that revolve around physical gratification.

The New Testament text does not use this word, but it is found in some classical Greek writings. It is such a low state of love that it is not even part of our New Testament writings. Erotic love is selfish by nature. It is concerned with pleasing the sensual appetites. When the Bible speaks of love, it never implies carnal fulfillment. *Eros* is not of the Lord and, in fact, is in direct opposition to true love. If it can even be classified as love, it is on the absolute opposite end of the spectrum from God's love. *Eros* is about gaining self-gratification and fulfillment of personal, physical, and sensual needs. This form of love is totally foreign to the love portrayed in the Scriptures. In the language of the New Testament, there is no *eros*; there is only *phileo* and *agape*.

PHILEO LOVE

The word *phileo* means to have ardent affection and feeling. It is an impulsive type of love. We can define *phileo* as a natural human affection, characterized by powerful feelings or sentiments. It brings with it much more of the emotional aspects of love.

Phileo is often used to express a familial type of love due to the sentimental qualities associated with the love of family. Scriptural language never uses *phileo* to designate God's love for man or even man's love for God. However, most people operate at this emotional level. Even many Christians operate on this base level of emotional, sentimental love. They talk about their relationship with God and how much they love Him. When you talk to them about their testimony, they most often talk about an emotional event from their past. While this is not the lowest level of love in the Greek language, it is the lowest in Scriptural language.

Phileo in Scripture

There is nothing wrong with having *phileo* love. Jesus Himself experienced *phileo* love. John tells us that Jesus loved Lazarus with this *phileo* type of love. John 11:3-6 records the event of Lazarus' death. "Therefore, the sisters sent to Him, saying, 'Lord, behold, he whom You love is sick' . . . Now Jesus loved Martha and her sister and Lazarus." The word here is *phileo*. He had a strong natural affection towards Lazarus.

Though it can, and often does, apply to brotherly love, *phileo* does not actually mean brotherly love. It simply means a natural affection. When it says that Jesus loved Lazarus, it does not mean that He loved him as His brother, but rather that He had strong affection toward him. In their experience together, they bonded and became friends. There are some people that you love more than others . . . people with whom you naturally connect. That is the concept of *phileo* love.

In attempting to explain the concept of *phileo* love, some have reduced its meaning to "brotherly love." However, that equation is too narrow and not entirely accurate. *Phileo* love only applies to brotherly love when the word "brother" is joined to it. The city of Philadelphia in the United States is accurately called the City of Brotherly Love. The name Philadelphia was formed by transliterating the Greek words *phileo* (meaning love) and *adelphos* (meaning brother). The love of a brother. Thus, Philadelphia is called the City of Brotherly Love.

Jesus uses the word *phileo* when He tells His followers, "He who loves father or mother more than Me is not worthy of Me. And he who loves son or daughter more than Me is not worthy of Me" (Matt 10:37). He that is naturally affectionate towards his mother or father more than Christ is not worthy of Christ. The statement is not that if you love your mother or father with phileo (affectionate love) more than you love Him with agape (God-love), then you are unworthy. He is simply saying that if you do not have a higher natural affection for Him than you have for your own mother and father or your own children, then you are not worthy of Him.

Jesus once tells His followers that "he who loves this life will lose it, but he who hates his life in this world will have eternal life" (John 12:25). The word He used in this statement is the word *phileo*. He who holds a high, natural affection towards life in the physical realm will miss genuine life. True, abundant living flows from the spiritual realm. Obviously, all of us love our life to one degree or another. No one is that excited about dying. What Jesus is warning against is holding on to this world's system of living with sentimentality and natural affection and missing the abundant life that flows from the love of God.

In Luke 9:23, Jesus tells us we must deny ourselves and take up our cross to follow Him. That is antithetical to loving (having ardent, natural affection) your own physical life. The book of Revelation says that the overcomers did not love their own lives to where they were willing to die for the Gospel. "And they overcame him by the blood of the Lamb and by the word of their testimony, and they did not love their lives to the death" (Rev 12:11). Their physical life was not as important to them as their walk with God. The Apostle Paul says, "I live, yet not I; but Christ liveth in me" (Gal 2:20 KJV).

Paul, in another place, says, "I am caught between a strait. To die and be with the Lord would be great for me. But, to stay here and be with you is better for you" (Phil 1:23-24, paraphrase). He is saying, "I do not love this physical life. I don't care. This world is not my home." He tells us in that passage that he does not know what he would choose. Then, he says, "But I think I'll stay and serve you." He died to loving his life because it would actually be better for him to die and be in the presence of the Lord in fullness. He sacrificed that which was good for him for that which was good for the people.

To not love one's life is strange thinking today. Service and sacrifice are almost taboo in the Church today. Seeker-friendly churches are quite popular and can be found in nearly every city in America. Many times, building a crowd is a larger goal than building the Kingdom. Many churches have become exciting, fast-paced places that people enjoy attending, but often for the wrong reasons. Part of the draw is that the service is only going to take an hour, so you are in and out before you know it. If your intention in going to church is to be entertained and to leave within an hour, you may have overlooked the true purpose of church life.

There is a lot of pressure in America to play that game. We have created a consumer mentality in the Church. People come into the church as consumers: here is what I want, here is what I am looking for in a church, here is where you can meet my needs. If the church was truly functioning spiritually, there would be no such thing as, "Here is what I am looking for in a church." The biblical principle is, "I am seeking the Lord about what I am to do. How can I serve in this church?"

The church should not be a place you attend for entertainment. Instead, it should be a place to challenge you and give you an opportunity for service. As you serve, you will be filled, and your faith will rise. When your fundamental desire is for that which appeals to your senses and entertains you, then this principle of loving (*phileo*) your life becomes a problem. Most problems people have with the church are not deep, spiritual matters. They are usually something as silly as the color of the paint or the sound of the music. Seldom is it about the church heading in the wrong direction spiritually.

How does our prosperity teaching fit into this? If you are following Jesus to get rich, you will never gain true prosperity. We come to Jesus because of who He is. In allowing Him to love us and us to love Him, prosperity flows. It is an exchange principle of giving and receiving. As partners in the Body of Christ, we give-get-give. We give, and as a result, we receive more blessings, enabling us to give more. It is an endless cycle of giving, getting, and giving. God is not telling us to not enjoy the things He has created for our pleasure. What He is saying is that those things should not hold any attachment to us.

Jesus teaches we are not to have too much natural affection for this life. It is that natural affection that creates the attachment to our heart. In fact, John 15:19 tells us that "If you were of the world, the world would love its own. Yet because you are not of the world, but I chose you out of the world, therefore the world hates you." The word "world" in this text is the Greek word *cosmos*.

We get our word cosmopolitan from this word. It means "this world's system." He does not mean that we are no longer living in this physical world. One look in the mirror proves you are of this world. We are not aliens in that sense. We are natural citizens here. He means, however, that we are not of this cosmos, this system of thinking. This system is a system of greed and

28

consumerism. God's system is a system of giving. His system is not one of consuming, but, rather, of communing. While the world's system is about what is in it for "me," God's system is about what is in it for other people. His system is a system of relationship and fellowship.

God's system does not fit with the world's system. Industry recognizes that service is essential. When you go to a restaurant or any place of business, they are not usually serving because they absolutely care about you. They are really serving you because they know it produces profitability for their business. Jesus tells us that we are not of that system. We are of the system that says, "I am going to serve you, no matter what." No matter what you do, I am going to love you. I am going to lay down my life for my friends, even if my friends do not act like my friends.

Jesus told His disciples that the rulers of this world flaunt their authority and use that authority to serve themselves. But His followers were not to follow that pattern. He told the disciples that if they wanted to be great in His kingdom, they would have to learn to serve others. In His kingdom, the one who serves the most is the greatest. The person who is the servant of all is the greatest leader in His kingdom.

Unlike the world's system, His system is a system of serving and giving. This system of which we are a part clearly proclaims, "I am going to serve you. No matter what you do or say, I am going to love you. I am going to lay down my life for my neighbors and anyone in need is my neighbor. I am not going to use my authority to force people to wash my feet. Quite the opposite is true. Because of this great affection I have for others — this great love that is in me . . . I am going to use my authority to wash other people's feet." By serving others, I follow in Christ's footsteps. This kind of love goes beyond the natural affection of *phileo* love. It can only spring from a deeper place.

AGAPE LOVE

The love required to meet Christ's demands is the greatest type of love. This highest of loves is expressed with the Greek word *agape*. This word denotes the deepest, most perfect kind of love. *Agape* love involves the emotions, but it is not emotional. It is a matter of resolve and purpose that springs from a sense of belonging. This love is a determined act of the will. It requires evaluation and a clear decision to seek out relationship. It is the kind of love that differentiates between courting a woman and marrying a woman.

In a relationship that is solely romantic, you date a person who makes you feel good. You enjoy being with that person and feel an emotional attachment. But over time, the flaws and imperfections of the person begin to appear. As time goes on, the flaws and peculiarities of the person you are dating begin to grate on your emotions. As that emotional attachment wanes, the relationship dies because you no longer receive the emotional satisfaction you once experienced.

Then one day, you meet that person who moves you out of the emotional, consumer realm. You are so enamored by this person that you love them despite the negatives. You cannot imagine life without that person and are determined to make it a lifelong relationship. In helping prepare young couples for marriage, we tell young couples, "The love required to make marriage successful is not merely an emotion. It is an act of the will. You must determine to live your life together forever." The moment you call it an emotion, you open the door to all sorts of problems. If you "fall" in love, you may just as easily "fall" out of love. True *agape* love is not something you fall into. It is planned and intentional – it is an act of the will. A judgment is made. You chose to love that person.

When Jesus spoke to His disciples about loving their neighbors, He used this word *agape*. The Lord does not tell us to have a natural, emotional affection (*phileo*) towards our neighbors. He tells us to *agape* our neighbors; to love them as an act of our will. He says, "You may not have a natural affection for your neighbor. He may be that person whom you can barely tolerate and with whom you have nothing in common. I am not telling you to have a natural affection towards your neighbor. I

30

am telling you—as an act of your will and your judgment—you are to love (agape) your neighbor." *Agape* is an intentional decision to love another person. However, it is impossible to know the depths of this love without divine revelation.

The translators of the King James Version translated this word, *agape*, as charity in 1 Corinthians 13. In the New Testament, translators translated both agape and phileo as "love," but only translated *agape* as "charity." By definition, charity speaks of affection and a tender, passionate attachment. Based on this definition, charity sounds more like what we have said about phileo than *agape*. But there is a very important, though subtle, difference between the two. Natural affection is *phileo*, whereas *agape* is willful affection. There are certain people you connect and bond with immediately. We all have those friends whom we feel like we have known forever. That is *phileo*—a natural attraction to another person. *Agape* is a similar, though deeper type of affection—but it is not natural. When He says that we are to *agape* our enemies, we are to have tender affection towards our enemies. But that is an unnatural affection. We must exercise our will to love that person.

On the other hand, this *agape* type of love is often instigated by the character and qualities of the other person. What we see in that person draws us to choose to love them. The qualities we see in that person command our affection. An example is our love for God. Discovering the character and attributes of God stimulates our affections towards Him, leading us to choose to enter into a love relationship with Him.

Many, if not most, Christians have a sentimental, emotional attachment to God and get warm, emotional feelings during certain church services. When the choir sings Handel's "Messiah" at Christmas time, we are moved to tears. Yet, when we leave the church service, we cannot sustain that emotion. Our relationship with God is tossed to and fro by our emotions. Sometimes, we feel like we love God and at other times, we don't. Our spiritual life is an emotional roller coaster. In that case, we are not operating in the willful *agape* type of love. When our love

31

springs from our emotions and natural affections, It is *phileo* love, rather than *agape.*

It is the loving character of our God that draws us into a deeper relationship than simple emotion and natural affection. God's desire is that we choose to love Him. When Jesus was asked the question about the greatest commandment, He did not hesitate. He simply repeated the age-old command, "You shall love the Lord your God with all your heart, with all your soul, with all your mind, and with all your strength" (Mark 12:30, Deut. 6:5). We are to love God with this *agape* love that is intentional and all-encompassing. Because of the intensity of the affections, it will always be foremost in the desires of the heart. Those love-desires will stimulate the mind to take up the course in full intensity. As the mind envisions the perfect fulfillment of those desires, the soul fully commits to the task of achieving those love-desires for relationship with Almighty God.

Agape in Scripture

When the apostle John writes in 1 John 4:16 that God is love, he uses this word *agape.* Our God is not some whimsical deity operating on self-gratifying impulse. No. The God of the Bible is purposeful, knowing the end and the beginning. Every action is a willful decision that moves His purposes one step closer to fulfillment. Everything He does or thinks is motivated by pure, unselfish love. Therefore, God-love is willful, intentional, and all-encompassing. God is *agape.*

Because it is God's love, *agape* love can be found all throughout the Scriptures. According to Jesus, operating in this *agape* love fulfills all the Law and the Prophets. The Jewish leaders of Jesus' day had serious difficulty grasping a kingdom based upon love. In their mind, the kingdom of God was about keeping the Law to attain righteousness. One day, one of the lawyers of the Pharisees asked Jesus a question about the Law. He was fully convinced that Jesus held the Law in contempt. So, the question was posed in hopes of exposing Jesus' true beliefs about the Law.

32

The lawyer asks, "Of all the laws given to us through Moses, which is most important? Which law must we be most conscious to obey to attain righteousness.?" Without hesitation, Jesus reaches back into the Law of Moses and quotes the Law to the Lawyer. The Lawyer was intimately acquainted with the story of Moses coming down from the mountain with the Ten Commandments in his hand. Moses read the commands to the children of Israel, but the people were afraid of the presence of God. So Moses instructed them that the most important thing is to love God. He said, "Hear, O Israel: The Lord our God, the Lord is one! You shall love the LORD your God with all your heart, with all your soul, and with all your strength" (Deut. 6:4-5).

The lawyer's confrontational question was answered with Moses' counsel. "You shall love the LORD your God with all your heart, with all your soul, and with all your mind.' This is the first and great commandment." That one summary command of Moses covered the first four commands of the Ten Commandments. The word translated "love" in this command is this word *agape*. If you *agape* God with all your being, you will fulfill the written commands without thought. To cover the other six laws of the Ten, Jesus quoted a much lesser-known command from the Levitical Law. It is found in a passage detailing the moral law given to Israel.

The passage speaks of leaving some of the harvest in the field for the poor to reap. This preserved the dignity of the poor. This was no handout. They had to go into the field and reap the "corners" of the harvest. Then, the passage moves to rules of how to treat your fellow man. Amid a long list of "Thou shall not's", we find a positive command. "You shall love your neighbor as yourself" (Lev 19:18). In Hebrew, this phrase consists of only three little words. Yet, Jesus says that all the Law hangs on these three little words and the command to love God. Jesus is clarifying that the kingdom of God is a kingdom of love. If we want to be a part of that kingdom, we must operate in *agape* love.

If we love God in this perfect love and love our neighbor in this perfect love, then we fulfill all the Law and the Prophets. He did not just say that the Ten Commandments are fulfilled when this love is expressed. He said that all the Law is fulfilled in loving God and loving your neighbor in this highest, perfect sense.

Agape love is the first named element in the "fruit of the Spirit" in Galatians 5:22: "But the fruit of the Spirit is love (*agape*)." When God's life forces flow through us, the first fruit produced is Love. Love is the first fruit to appear because God is love. This is the first evidence that the Holy Spirit has taken control of us.

Jesus stood over Jerusalem and wept over the city. This is the same Jerusalem that would soon scream, "Crucify Him! Crucify Him!" Jesus knew that the people that He came to save were going to turn against Him. Yet, it broke His heart that they would do such a thing. Imagine that scene in the garden when Judas kissed Jesus on the cheek. There was great love coming out of Jesus, even for Judas. Jesus says, "Judas, will you betray Me with a kiss?" There was hurt and pain in that statement. Love was violated at that moment. There was no bitterness or hatefulness in Jesus' voice, nor was there a rebuke. There was simply love for His enemies. When Jesus, on the cross, cries out, "Father, forgive them; they know not what they do" He was expressing the God-love that was in Him. Above all else, He loved.

As stated earlier, the King James Version of the Bible translates *agape* with the word charity. A further look at this word charity may help us grasp the depth of *agape* love. Charity means to think or speak well of others or to judge their actions in a kind and considerate way. The object of charity is to make others happy. It also means to be generous to the poor. *Agape* embodies each of these actions. When we begin to grasp a full understanding of *agape* love, we will begin operating in that place of pure love. We, too, will look at others and judge with kindness, rather than with vengeance. We sill begin speaking well of others. Our mouths will speak blessings and not judgment upon those around us.

Because we are filled with the God of Love, we were created in love and intended to walk in love. In John 13:35, Jesus says that people will know that we are His disciples by our love, our *agape* love. People will know that we are followers of Christ because we operate at a love level above all others. James, the brother of Jesus, writes, "out of the same mouth proceed blessings and curses—these things should not be" (James 3:10, paraphrase). Blessings, not curses, should flow out of the mouths of the people of God. Paul later reminds us to "bless those who persecute you, bless and do not curse" (Rom 12:14). We are not a cursing people; we are a blessing people. We are a people of love. How can that which is of love curse? When we understand God's unending, unconditional love for us, this love verbiage and actions will become natural to us.

The thoughts of God toward us give birth to agape love. Jeremiah 29:11 states, "For I know the thoughts that I think toward you, says the LORD, thoughts of peace and not of evil, to give you a future and a hope." God has good thoughts for you! David says, "Such thoughts are too high for me; I cannot attain to them" (Ps 139:6 paraphrase). These deep, constant interests and positive feelings of God are towards us. Man is the only recipient of the *agape* love of God. *W. E. Vine's, An Expository Dictionary of Biblical Words*[3] , gives us this summary definition of *agape*: "In respect of *agapao* as used of God, it expresses the deep and constant 'love' and interest of a perfect Being towards entirely unworthy objects, producing and fostering a reverential 'love' in them towards the Giver, and a practical 'love' towards those who are partakers of the same, and a desire to help others to seek the Giver."

This perfect love is bestowed upon us, despite our unworthiness. We must acknowledge that unworthiness, but we cannot dwell on it. We are unworthy to receive it, but once we receive it, we become worthy. If you have an old car that is only

---

[3] W. E. Vine's, An Expository Dictionary of Biblical Words, Copyright © 1996 by Thomas Nelson Publishers. All rights reserved. Used by permission.

worth five hundred dollars, and I offer you five thousand dollars for it, the car is now worth five thousand dollars. It is no longer worth five hundred. This is exactly what God says. We are unworthy, but the moment He puts His bid in, we become worthy. We were unworthy to receive His love, but He gave us His love. Romans 5:8 tells us that "God demonstrates His own love toward us, in that while we were still sinners, Christ died for us." The moment He died for us, that which was unworthy became worthy. Now, according to the writer of Hebrews, we have the right to "come boldly to the throne of grace" (Heb 4:16). His love and grace are sufficient to cover every sin. Because of His grace, we are made worthy of His love. His grace gives us what we do not deserve—His *agape* (intentional) love for us!

When we receive these good thoughts and unconditional love, it creates loving, reverential thoughts and feelings in us towards God, the Giver of this love, and towards other people. Most relationships begin with a lover and a recipient. It is hard to resist loving someone if they keep loving you. Their love for you produces a love for them in you.

It is as though God says, "They do not love Me, so I am going to love them. I am going to overwhelm them with My love. My extravagant love for them will create a love for Me in them." That idea is expressed in 1 John 4:19. "Not that we first loved Him, but He loved us and gave His son for us" (paraphrase). He did not wait for us to love Him. Just like in creation, His love is proactive. What a perfect picture of *agape* love.

Agape and 1 Corinthians

We find a summary definition of *agape* love in 1 Corinthians 13:4-8. The Message gives us a good interpretation of these defining words.

Love never gives up
Love cares more for others than for self
Love doesn't want what it doesn't have
Love doesn't strut
Doesn't have a swelled head

Doesn't force itself on others
Isn't always "me first"
Doesn't fly off the handle
Doesn't keep score of the sins of others
Doesn't revel when others grovel.
Takes pleasure in the flowering of truth
Puts up with anything
Trusts God always
Always looks for the best
Never looks back,
But keeps going to the end
Love never dies.

With that definition in mind, consider Matthew 22:37-40: "Jesus said to him, 'You shall love the LORD your God with all your heart, with all your soul, and with all your mind. This is the first and great commandment. And the second is like it: You shall love your neighbor as yourself. On these two commandments hang all the Law and the Prophets."

We are to *agape* the LORD our God with all our heart, soul, and mind. This means loving Him with an infinite love that cares more about Him than ourselves. It means loving Him with a love that does not want what it does not have. Many Christians love God while wanting what they do not have. They are asking God to help them get more. We should rejoice in what we have. But so many Christians feel dissatisfied. They cannot enjoy what they have because they are lusting after the things that they do not have. Love says, "Learn to be content. Learn to be excited with just Me and Thee."

Remember, God does not stop at our love between Himself and us. We are also to *agape* our neighbor in the same way that He loves us. We are to love our neighbors with this *agape* love that "does not revel when others grovel," "does not fly off the handle", is not always saying – me first, and "does not keep score of the sins of others". It is a sacrificial, other-serving love. The truth is that man can never develop this kind of love. It must be given to Him by the God of love. For this reason, Galatians 5:22

lists *agape* love as the first fruit of the Spirit. This *agape* love is found in the branches that are securely attached to the Vine. The life forces of the Vine flow through the branch and the strongest of forces is *agape* love.

THE PROCESS

When we abide in Christ, we experience His presence—the very presence of Love itself. It is then that we truly experience His love. Zephaniah 3:17 says: "The LORD your God in your midst, the Mighty One, will save; He will rejoice over you with gladness, He will quiet you with His love, He will rejoice over you with singing." Notice that it says that God will do the singing. It is not that you will sing to Him. He sings to you!

As we abide in Christ, we begin to hear His love song to us. We begin to hear Him whisper sweet nothings in our ear, telling us how good we are and how much He loves us. When your Lover (Jesus) expresses His love to you, nothing else matters. Once you come to the realization of God's deep, unending, unconditional love for you, a new thing is birthed inside of you. You have a new life source. Confidence and boldness rise within you.

When you learn to hear His voice, it does not matter what the world brings. Confidence will rise in you because you know that your Father loves you and has all things in His control. We express this *agape* love to God and to others around us. When it becomes real to us, we can love the LORD our God with all our heart, mind, and soul. Only then will we be able to express this love of God to other people. If we miss *agape*, we have missed it all. For this reason, Mark 8:36 asks, "For what will it profit a man if he gains the whole world, and loses his own soul?"

The soul is the seat of the mind, the will, and the emotions. *Agape* love flows out of the soul. It is an act of the will that creates and carries with it strong emotions. But it is much more than some natural attraction. This *agape* type of love is the willful act of our soul. Our Creator created us with free will so that our love for Him would not be a forced thing. In response to the goodness of God, we choose to use that free will to love Him.

With this understanding, return to 1 Corinthians 13 and read this hymn of love. Remember the word used here is *agape*:

> *Though I speak with the tongues of men and of angels, but have not agape love* (willful choosing to love God and others), *I have become sounding brass or a clanging cymbal. And though I have the gift of prophecy, and understand all mysteries and all knowledge, and though I have all faith, so that I could remove mountains, but have not love* (willful, unselfish love for God and others), *I am nothing. And though I bestow all my goods to feed the poor, and though I give my body to be burned, but have not* (this perfect, highest, willful agape) *love, it profits me nothing. Love* (agape) *suffers long and is kind; love* (agape) *does not envy; love* (agape) *does not parade itself, is not puffed up; does not behave rudely, does not seek its own, is not provoked, thinks no evil; does not rejoice in iniquity, but rejoices in the truth; bears all things, believes all things, hopes all things, endures all things. Love* (agape) *never fails. But whether there are prophecies, they will fail; whether there are tongues, they will cease; whether there is knowledge, it will vanish away. For we know in part and we prophesy in part. But when that which is perfect has come, then that which is in part will be done away. When I was a child, I spoke as a child, I understood as a child, I thought as a child; but when I became a man, I put away childish things. For now we see in a mirror, dimly, but then face to face. Now I know in part, but then I shall know just as I also am known. And now abide faith, hope, love* (highest, unselfish, willful, predetermined act of love), *these three; but the greatest of these is* (agape) *love.* (emphasis added)

We opened this chapter with the story of Jesus sharing breakfast with the apostles. As we examine His conversation with Peter, our understanding of the different types of love gives us greater revelation from the passage. If you remember, after breakfast, Jesus asked Peter, "Do you love me?" Peter responded, "Yes, Lord, you know that I love you." When Jesus asked the question, he used the word *agape*. But when Peter responded, he used the word *phileo*. Peter was asked if he loved Jesus unconditionally with that deep God kind of love, and Peter responded that he was fond of Jesus. Jesus repeats the question using the same wording and Peter responds again with *phileo*.

For a third and final time, Jesus asked Peter if he loved Him. But this time He uses the word *phileo*. In essence, Jesus is saying, "Peter, you say that you *phileo* Me. But do you really even love Me with natural affection like you love your family." John 21:17 says that this third question grieved Peter. Jesus was questioning the depth of his love. I wonder if He might ask us the same question.

And now abide faith, hope, love, these three; but the greatest of these is love
1 Corinthians 13:13.

3
LOVE GOD

*Once the seeking heart finds God in personal experience
there will be no further problem about loving him. To
know him is to love him and to know him better is to love
him more*
—A. W. Tozer

To love God and to be loved by God is the essence of human existence. There is no level of human life higher than a love relationship with God. When God conceived the very idea of mankind, He had this relationship in mind. He understood that this creation would be totally different from all other creations. This creation must manifest the character and life of the Creator if there was to be relationship.

So, God created us in His very image and likeness and gave us relationship at a level no other creature experiences. When God breathed His very life into Adam, He elevated humanity to a level of existence yet unknown. This was a creation that could walk in the Garden with God in the cool of the day. This was a creation that could be the recipient of His love. With this creation, a whole new level of loving relationship was initiated. This relationship was elevated to the level of fellowship. This was the very purpose for the creation of humans. We were created to love and to be loved.

When God created humans in His own image and likeness, He established this loving relationship. This creation in His own image and likeness was like no other -- for God is like no other.

This creation possessed God's spiritual DNA. This creation was the very image of the Father. All the heavenly host must have stood in awe as Almighty God formed this creature into His self-portrait. This creation was the perfect representation of God dwelling in the physical realm.

In that image and likeness, there is a perplexity. God is so totally unique that He stands in solitary aloneness. Being in His exact image, man, too, was created totally alone. Nothing is comparable to God or is even directly relatable to Him other than man. Even His angels cover their faces in the awful awesomeness of His holy presence. As they look upon the awesomeness of His presence, they proclaim, "Holy, Holy, Holy is the Lord God Almighty!"

When we join with them and speak or sing of the holiness of God, we are actually alluding to this absolute uniqueness. The word translated as "holy" literally means "wholly other." To say that God is holy is to say that God is totally outside of any earthly experience or comparison. He is wholly other; so wholly different that there is nothing with which to compare Him. Since man was created in the very image and likeness of God, he also possessed that "wholly other" characteristic. Man is totally distinct from all other created beings. Our "image and likeness" of God makes us spirit beings totally unique in the created order. We are God's unique imagers dwelling in this physical realm.

But with that uniqueness comes that solitary aloneness that God Himself experienced. With every act of creation, God paused and surveyed His handiwork. As He surveyed each day's creation, He exclaimed, "It is good." But when God surveyed man, He did not say, "It is good." In realizing that He had created man in that aloneness of otherness, He exclaimed, "It is not good. It is not good that man should dwell in that loneness of uniqueness. I will make a partner for him. Together, they will love me and love each other."

In the 12th chapter of Mark's gospel, Jesus stresses the importance of this love relationship. A young Pharisee lawyer asked Jesus which of the commandments was foremost. We

Gentiles tend to think of the Ten Commandments as the totality of God's commands. But such was not the case for this young scribe. He would have clearly been thinking of the Mitzvah as outlined in the Book of Commandments. This work consisted of 613 commandments (mitzvah) or individual commands. These 613 commandments were divided into two sections. 365 of these commands were positive commands: "Thou shalt" commands. The remaining 248 of the commands were negative in nature: "Thou shat not" commands.

The Jewish lawyers took great delight in arguing which of these commands carried the greatest importance. This question was much like the juvenile theological question, "How many angels can dance on the head of a pen?" These scribes believed that all 613 of the mitzvah were important and must be kept. However, they assumed some commands carried more importance than others. Because the 613 individual commands were quite burdensome, they continually tried to concoct a summary law that fulfilled the whole.

So, the question of the scribe was not a frivolous question. This was a question that he would have debated many times. Just moments earlier, both Pharisees and Sadducees had attempted to ensnare Christ with trick questions. Designed to put Jesus at odds with Rome, the Pharisees asked a baited question about the legality of paying taxes to Caesar.

The Sadducees' exaggerated question about the resurrection was absurd. The Sadducees didn't even believe in the resurrection. So, Jesus' answer to their ludicrous riddle is laced with ridicule and sarcasm. His answer strikes at the very heart of their question. Jesus says, "You're asking of these ridiculous questions proves you don't understand the Scriptures, much less how the spirit realm operates."

The scribe, now addressing Christ, had listened to His response to these questions and was impressed with His answer. To him it seemed to be an opportune time to ask the Rabbi's opinion of which of the commands carried the most weight. Maybe the Rabbi could settle this age-old debate. Maybe he could get an authoritative answer as to which type was most important—the positive or the negative. Should the "Thou shalt" laws be given first place in importance or the "Thou shall not" commands?

We must assume that Jesus believed the man to be sincere, for there is no hint of rebuke in his answer. Apparently, Jesus senses that this man is serious in asking the question. As a scribe, the man is very familiar with the law, and he simply desires to know Jesus' opinion. Jesus gives him a simple and straightforward answer. Without a moment's hesitation, Jesus quotes Deuteronomy 6:4-5. "Hear, O Israel: The Lord our God, the Lord is one! You shall love the Lord your God with all your heart, with all your soul, with all your mind, and with all your strength." You must love God with the totality of your being.

THE GREAT COMMANDMENT

As Jesus gave His answer, this student of the Law would have immediately recognized the words. As Jesus begins His answer, you can imagine this loyal Jew reciting the words with Him. "Hear, O Israel: The Lord our God, the Lord is one! You shall love the Lord your God with all your heart, with all your soul, with all your mind, and with all your strength." After all, he personally quoted these words twice a day, every day of his life. Every morning and evening, he recited the "Shema".

The Shema gets its name from the first Hebrew word of the proclamation and means to "hear" or "listen". On the Day of Atonement, the "Shema" is the high point of the priestly proclamation on this holiest of days. It affirms the fact that God is the one and only God. It calls the Jewish people to an all-consuming love for God.

Even though the opening line of the Shema is not provided, both He and the scribe were familiar with the words. They understood that "Hear, O Israel" did not simply mean to listen in the sense of merely hearing the words. The word Shema means something much deeper. It means to listen and understand to the point of prompting an action. So, the concept of the hearing expressed in the Shema is to hear to the point of taking action.

In our last lesson, we learned that the highest form of love is agape love. This is the Greek word Jesus uses when He says, "You shall love the Lord your God with all your heart, with all your soul, with all your mind, and with all your strength." Even though the original text records the words in Greek, Jesus would clearly have quoted the Shema from the Hebrew. In Hebrew, the word is *ahavah*. This word helps us understand *agape* love. For *ahavah* is not some simple emotional feeling. *Ahavah* is a commitment of fidelity and faithfulness. This love is a love in action.

To *ahavah* (love) the Lord was to faithfully keep the covenant and obey the Mitzvah. By the time of Christ, the Pharisees had turned the Law into a legalistic endeavor designed to gain God's favor. But that was never the intent of God's commandments. When Israel loved God and listened to the voice of God, they would walk in the blessings of God. To truly "*ahavah*" God, they would have to listen to His instructions and respond in obedience.

When we enter into this kind of love relationship with God, we joyfully listen to His commands. We love Him so much that we desire to hear His counsel and walk in His ways because we understand His goodness. We keep His commandments because we love Him so deeply. Jesus made this same connection of love and obedience in John 14:21. "He who has My commandments and keeps them, it is he who loves Me. And he who loves Me will be loved by My Father, and I will love him and manifest Myself to him." He further explained this connection two verses later, when He told His disciples, "If anyone loves Me, he will keep My word; and My Father will love him, and We will come to him and make Our home with him. He who does not love Me does not keep My words; and the word which you hear is not Mine but the Father's who sent Me."

When Jesus answers the scribe with the Shema, He is saying that the most important thing is to love God with the entirety of our being. Everything we are, everything we have, and everything we ever will be is designed to love God. We love Him to the extent that our very behavior is affected. We are to *agape (ahavah)* God with all our heart, soul, mind, and strength.

This kind of love has as its greatest desire to enter into a loving fellowship with God. In Revelation 3:20, Jesus tells us He stands at the door and knocks. He calls us into this fellowship of love. He goes on to say that if we hear His voice and open the door, we will have fellowship with Him. He is calling us into that close, intimate fellowship of agape love. 1 Corinthians 1:9 states that we have been "called into the fellowship of His Son." Jesus calls this loving fellowship eternal life. In His high priestly prayer of John 17, Jesus prays, "This is eternal life, that they may know You, the only true God, and Jesus Christ whom You have sent."

This fellowship is founded and grounded upon a grateful expression and high esteem of our God and His goodness. What other god loves his people and makes sacrifice for them? Other gods demand sacrifice and are feared by their followers. Only our God seeks a deep, loving relationship with His people. No other religion to which I am familiar is founded upon the love and goodness of their god. As believers, we obey the voice of God not out of legalistic obligation, but because we take delight in obeying Him. No wonder Jesus' answer is so simple. "Love your God with your whole being."

Jesus' answer to the Pharisees and Sadducees had impressed the scribe. Now, he approves Jesus' assessment of what is most important in the Law. The light of revelation has begun to shine in his heart. In honest admiration, the scribe replies, "That is a brilliant answer, Teacher. To love God with all your being and love others as yourself is more important than all the ceremonial law."

This is quite a compliment, coming from this one who has given his life to the law. Remember, there are no copy machines in those days. This man spent his life manually copying the

Scriptures word for word. He was intimately acquainted with the Scriptures. Pleased with his response and recognizing the Light bursting forth, Jesus says to him, "You are not far from the kingdom of God."

Since these words of Jesus so impressed the scribe, let us think for a moment as to the significance of loving God with all our being. As Moses was giving the Law to the children of Israel, he instructed the people to be careful to obey all that the Lord had instructed. He was not trying to restrict them. He was attempting to liberate them. If they heeded the voice of their God, all would go well with them. They were on the journey to the land that God had promised them: a land flowing with milk and honey. If they were to fully experience the fullness of this provision, they must enter into this love relationship with the totality of their being—heart, soul, and strength.

This love is a determination of the will. It is so high that it must always include choice. God in no way wants to force His love on us or make us love Him without choice. That would not be the relationship He desires. He gives us the ability to choose not to love Him so that our love for Him will be pure. This is a personalized love. "You shall love the Lord, your God." Notice the command is to love YOUR God. You must decide to love your God to the point that you willingly and joyfully obey His commands.

THE GREAT OBJECT OF OUR LOVE

A grand object worthy of that love must be the foundation of this great commandment to love. How can we not love the One who loved us so much that He sacrificed His Son for us? And how can we not love the One who laid down His very life for us? This choice to love God is not some whimsical, emotional choice. Once we understand the worthiness of the Object of this commandment, the choice is an obvious act of our will.

The choice becomes blatantly clear when we understand the "riches of His goodness, forbearance, and longsuffering towards us" (Rom 2:4). For it is the goodness of God that draws us into this love relationship. When Moses asked to see God's glory, God responded, "I will make all My goodness pass before you, and I will proclaim the name of the Lord before you. I will be gracious to whom I will be gracious, and I will have compassion on whom I will have compassion" (Ex 33:19). His very nature is one of infinite goodness. When the first couple ate of the Tree of Knowledge of Good and Evil, they lost their absolute goodness. They lost their God-likeness. God is only goodness. Jesus proclaimed, "No one is good but One, that is, God" (Matt 19:17).

The Psalmist praises the goodness of God when he writes, "Let them praise the name of the Lord, For His name alone is exalted; His glory is above the earth and heaven" (Ps 148:13). His glory (goodness) far surpasses anything we can see or imagine in this realm. We have nothing to which we can compare the glory of His goodness. We only know partial goodness, maybe great displays of goodness, but not absolute goodness. His goodness is absolute. In his letter to the church, James explains God's absolute goodness. He writes, "Every good gift and every perfect gift is from above, and comes down from the Father of lights, with whom there is no variation or shadow of turning" (Jas 1:17).

When the Psalmist says to praise the name of the Lord, he is letting us know that the names of God reveal His goodness. He praises God for who He is as revealed in the names given unto Him. So let us take a moment to review the greatness of this object of our love as revealed in His names. Space will not permit the extended list of names. So, we will only concentrate on a few. With those few, we will begin to see the vast goodness of our God.

Our God is not just any god, He is the God Most High. David declares, "You, Lord, are most high above all the earth; You are exalted far above all gods" (Psalm 97:9). In Genesis 14, we find the story of Abram paying tribute to Melchizedek. Abram had just rescued Lot by defeating the five invading kings. With no introduction, Melchizedek, the king of Salem (peace), appears on the scene. He is called the priest of *El Elyon* -- the God Most

High. In the ancient Biblical Hebrew language, there were no superlatives. There is no word for "highest". So, in his blessing of Abram, Melchizedek said, "Blessed be Abram of God Most High, Possessor of heaven and earth; And blessed be God Most High, Who has delivered your enemies into your hand" (Gen 14:19-20). This highest of gods, who is the possessor of everything, is our deliverer and protector. Without limitation or hesitation, He is indeed the worthy object of our love.

Just three chapters later, we find an even deeper revelation of this object of our love. God is promising Abram an heir: a son of his own body. To strengthen Abram's faith, God adds a new name - *El Shaddai*. God says, "I am Almighty God; walk before Me and be blameless. And I will make My covenant between Me and you and will multiply you exceedingly" (Gen 17:1-2). The name translated Almighty God is the Hebrew, *El Shaddai*. The word *El* simply means God. Although we cannot say with absolute certainty, it appears that the word *Shaddai* comes from the root word *shad* which means breast. As a mother nourishes, supplies, and protects her baby. Everything the infant needs to grow and be healthy is provided at the mother's breast. God is telling Abram that everything he needs is provided by this "All Sufficient One." In His goodness, He provides everything we need. In 2 Corinthians 12:9, the Lord tells Paul that His grace is sufficient for him. The Lord is simply reiterating that He is *El Shaddai* – the All Sufficient One.

Jesus addresses this concept in the Sermon on the Mount. He tells the disciples not to worry about the essentials of life. He says, "Your heavenly Father knows that you need all these things. But seek first the kingdom of God and His righteousness, and all these things shall be added to you" (Matt 6:32-33). Paul makes it ever more clear in Philippians 4:19, when he writes, "My God shall supply all your need according to His riches in glory by Christ Jesus." What a perfect explanation of *El Shaddai*. Our sufficiency is in Him. That fact alone elicits great love from us. But the revelation is not nearly complete.

After the birth of Isaac, God reveals the depths of His sufficiency to Abraham. The revelation begins with a command that seems contradictory to goodness. God requests Abraham to make the most painful sacrifice imaginable. "Take now your son, your only son Isaac, whom you love, and go to the land of Moriah, and offer him there as a burnt offering on one of the mountains of which I shall tell you" (Gen 22:2). Knowing the goodness and sufficiency of his God, Abraham obeys immediately. Early the next morning, they make their way up Mt. Moriah. As they make their ascent, Isaac asks his father a logical question.

Isaac says, "Father, I see the wood for the altar. And I see the fire, but shouldn't we have brought a lamb?"

Abraham's response reveals the depth of his trust in the goodness of his God. He tells his son, "Don't worry, son, God will provide the lamb. He will provide the sacrifice for Himself." Abraham's confidence in God's sufficiency was so strong that he even believed God would raise Isaac from the dead if the sacrifice was completed. But such extremes were unnecessary. As Abraham raised his knife over Isaac's chest, the messenger of God called his name. He told Abraham not to harm his son. The necessary sacrifice was caught in the thicket behind him. Abraham rejoiced and called the place *Jehovah Jireh* – the Lord our provider. No matter how difficult the situation, *Jehovah Jireh* is always there to make provision.

Do you notice the progression in the revelation? First, this god is the God Most High. The Highest of Things (*El Elyon*). He exists before all things and all things exist through Him. As the Creator of All, He is the All-Sufficient One (*El Shaddai*). As the All-Sufficient One, He is the Lord our Provider (*Jehovah Jireh*). *Jehovah Jireh* is the first of many compound names of our God that reveal His desire and ability to meet every need. The first and greatest of these provisions is the supplying of the sacrifice.

Unlike the other gods of the earth who require sacrifice from their worshippers, our God supplies the sacrifice for us. Think of those prophetic words of John the Baptist when he saw Jesus approaching along the shores of the Jordan River. "Look! Here He is. The Lamb of God that takes away the sin of the world." A few short years later, they sacrificed Jesus on that hill outside of Jerusalem known as Golgotha. These are the very same mountains upon which God supplied the sacrifice for Abraham – Moriah. As surely as He supplied the sacrifice for Abraham, He supplied the sacrifice for us. This ultimate sacrifice of God's own Son is the definitive expression of God's goodness.

The second of the compound names of God is *Jehovah Raphe*. Approximately sixty times, the Old Testament uses the word *raphe*. It always speaks of healing, remedy, or restoration. Not only does it involve healing in the physical realm, but in the moral and spiritual realm as well. Moses liberated Israel from Egypt by way of the powerful plagues of God. Then God provided their final deliverance by drowning Pharoah's army in the Red Sea. But then came the long march towards Canaan. During a time of perplexity and need, *Jehovah Jireh*, manifests Himself as *Jehovah Raphe* – the Lord our Healer.

Israel began the journey with great confidence and joy. God had taken notice of their condition and had provided deliverance. In Exodus 15, we find their exuberant song of praise and thanksgiving for all that God had done. With heartfelt gratitude, they proclaim, "The Lord is my strength and song, And He has become my salvation; He is my God, and I will praise Him; My father's God, and I will exalt Him." With that song in their heart, they set out through the wilderness following their Deliverer. But the heat of the desert sun soon began to drain their enthusiasm. By day 3 of their journey, their temperament had changed. They were hot and tired, and more importantly, they had run out of water.

One can only imagine the excitement these thirsty travelers must have experienced as they saw an oasis in the desert. Running and plunging headlong into the water, they would most likely have joyfully filled their mouth with the water. But their tongues must have curled as the rusty pipe taste of this heavy water dried out their already dry mouths. It is easy for us to disdain their ingratitude, but thirst is a powerful force. They cry out to Moses for an answer, "What do we do now? We can't drink this water and there doesn't appear to be any other source for miles." Imagine the despair the mothers must have felt as they looked down upon their children crying in voiceless dryness.

In the midst of this desperate situation, Moses cries out to God. He has no answer in himself, so he calls on the All-Sufficient, Most High God for provision. The Lord points him to a specific tree and instructs him to throw a limb of that tree into the waters. How silly that must have sounded to Moses. One tree limb is going to change the chemical makeup of the spring. But desperate times call for desperate action. Moses did as the Lord commanded, and instantly, the waters changed.

The Scriptures tell us that the waters became sweet. One can only imagine how their mood must have instantly reversed. One minute their mouths are full of the most awful tasting liquid ever to cross human lips. The next moment, they are gulping down the sweetest water ever consumed by man. In that moment of satisfaction ecstasy, the Lord makes them a promise and reveals a little more of Himself to them. He proclaims, "If you diligently heed the voice of the Lord your God and do what is right in His sight, give ear to His commandments and keep all His statutes, I will put none of the diseases on you which I have brought on the Egyptians. For I am the Lord who heals you – I am Jehovah Raphe" (Ex 15:26, explanation adds).

Decades later, David praises God for his healing character when he sings, "Bless the Lord, O my soul; And all that is within me, bless His holy name! Bless the Lord, O my soul, And forget not all His benefits: Who forgives all your iniquities, Who heals all your diseases" (Ps 103:1-3). He is the Lord our Healer, who heals all our infirmities, both spiritual and physical. He takes away our sins and our sickness and pain.

In his prophecy about the coming Messiah, the prophet Isaiah speaks of this healing virtue. The Complete Jewish Bible gives us a very descriptive translation of the prophet's words. "In fact, it was our diseases he bore, our pains from which he suffered; yet we regarded him as punished, stricken and afflicted by God. But he was wounded because of our crimes, crushed because of our sins; the disciplining that makes us whole fell on him, and by his bruises (stripes) we are healed" (Is 53:5-6). By His death on the cross, He has made us whole. He was and is *Jehovah Raphe*; the Lord our Healer. He heals our sins and our diseases. The greater our revelation of the depths of His provision for us, the greater our love for Him.

As *Jehovah Raphe*, Christ laid down His life for us. With His death on the cross, He purchased our healing and forgiveness. In 1 Peter 2:24, Peter writes that we were healed by His stripes –by His scourging. Then he states that we were like sheep running around with no purpose.

Sheep need a shepherd, and God revealed Himself as *Jehovah Rohi* or *Jehovah Raah*—the Lord our Shepherd. Both of the Hebrew words *rohi* and *raah* mean shepherd and are used interchangeably. Christ came as the Good Shepherd that brings us back to the Father. He came to give us life by laying down His life for us. As the Good Shepherd, He leads us to eternal life, for He is Life. In John 14:6, Jesus says, "I am the way, the truth, and the life. No one comes to the Father except through me." As our shepherd, He leads us to the Father, and our relationship with the Father gives us eternal life. In John 17:3, Jesus says, "And this is eternal life, that they may know You, the only true God, and Jesus Christ whom You have sent."

But long before Jesus came as the perfect expression of the Lord our Shepherd, God revealed Himself to Israel as *Jehovah Rohi* (or *Jehovah Raah*). The LORD led Israel through the wilderness as a shepherd leads his flock. Israel was a pastoral people and understood the characteristics of a shepherd. In reality, virtually all the revelations of the nature of God are seen in the idea of a good shepherd. Who better to lay that revelation out before us than David, the shepherd? Psalms 23 portrays the Lord our Shepherd as the summation of God's character. David begins with the words, "The LORD is my Shepherd." The original Hebrew simply declares *Yahweh Raah*.

So let us look deeper into that name, *Yahweh Raah* or *Jehovah Raah*. The basic meaning of *Yahweh* (Jehovah) comes from the Hebrew word *Havah*. *Havah* means "to exist" and implies "to become known" or "reveal existence." You remember the story of Moses and the burning bush. Moses asks the Lord, "Who shall I say sent me?" God responds with the name *Yahweh*. He tells Moses to say, "The I AM sent me."

The Hebrew word *raah* is the word for shepherd. The shepherd cares for his sheep by leading them to water and grass, as well as protecting them from predators. So, *Yahweh Raah* is the Self-Existent Shepherd. Who cannot resist the call to deep love and admiration when hearing David's words in Psalm 23? But there is much more revelation in this short Psalm than meets the eye. In these six short verses, David reveals the splendor of the covenant name of God.

The Lord is my shepherd
(Yahweh Raah);

I shall not want
(He is my sufficiency—El Shaddai).

He makes me to lie down in green pastures; He leads me beside the still waters.
(He is my peace—Yahweh Shalom).

He restores my soul;
(He is my healer—Yahweh Raphe)

He leads me in the paths of righteousness For His name's sake
(He is my righteousness—Yahweh Tsidkenu).

Yea, though I walk through the valley of the shadow of death, I will fear no evil; For You are with me; Your rod and Your staff, they comfort me.
(He is with me—Yahweh Shammah;
His military banner is over me—Yahweh Nissi).

You prepare a table before me in the presence of my enemies;
(He is my provider—Yahweh Yireh—Jehovah Jireh),

You anoint my head with oil
*(*He sets me apart and I am anointed—Yahweh M'Kaddesh*);*

My cup runs over.
(He provides in abundance — El Shadai).

Surely goodness and mercy shall follow me All the days of my life; And I will dwell in the house of the Lord forever.
(He is my Shepherd, Yahweh Raah and He provides a safe dwelling place with His presence).

The object of our love is indeed worthy of our love. He is the shepherd of our soul. In John 10, Jesus identifies Himself with this name and lays out His purpose in coming to earth. He tells His disciples that He came to bring life and bring so much life that it overflowed in abundance. He informs them that He is the Good Shepherd who gives His life so that they may have this abundance of life. How can we not love our God, who shepherds us into this abundance of life?

As we conclude this discussion of the grand object of our love, let us not slight the most important word in this command to love God. He does not command us to simply love a god. A personal relationship is being addressed. You are to love your God. In the same way we love our spouse, mother, father, children, etc., we are to love our God. A simple story from the history of Rome illustrates this concept vividly. One of the empire's emperors was returning to Rome in triumphant. He was surrounded by soldiers and military commanders as he made his ascent up the Appian Way.

Suddenly, a young boy broke through the military ranks and raced towards the emperor. As the story goes, one officer blocked his way and said, "I am sorry lad, but you cannot go up there. That is the emperor." Undaunted, the child darted past the officer. Over his shoulder, he responded, "He may be your emperor, but he is my father."

The object of our great love may simply be a god to others. But to us, his children, He is our Father God. He loved us while we were still sinners. Because of His great love for us, He sacrificed His life for us, forgave our sins, and brought us into His family. How marvelous, how wonderful is our Father's love for us. This revelation produces an all-encompassing love in us.

THE GREATEST LOVE

When Jesus told the scribe that he must love the Lord, He was careful in His word selection. He chose to use that word that speaks of unconditional, unselfish love—agape love. We were created to have a warm, personal affection for our God. We are to love Him with an undivided love. We are to agape Him. In the last chapter, we learned that agape is not just an emotional affection. It is a determined act of the will. It is giving the totality of our being to another. To give less than your all to the covenant is a failure to honor your pledge. The great love we express to our God must be unconditional and undivided. It must not be a wistful, divided thing. The love for God commanded here is willful, intentional, and all-encompassing. We are to love the Lord our God with the totality of our being: heart, soul, mind, and strength.

Love the LORD Your God With All Your Heart

When we see the word heart, we might assume that it refers to the blood-pumping muscle in the center of our chest. But when the Bible refers to the heart, it has a much deeper and varied meaning. However, the physical heart helps illustrate the complex and diverse usages. The heart is the central organ of the body. When the heart stops pumping, death is upon us. Without the heart's activity, life ceases. Because of this vital function, the word has come to stand for the center of our moral, spiritual, and emotional life.

When we speak of a soldier or athlete that has "heart", we are not speaking of physical organ, for every person has one of those.

We are speaking of something that comes from deep inside—from the very essence of that person. It is that quality that causes them to perform beyond normal expectations. Heart is that essence that gives us personality and character. It speaks of the innermost qualities that make us who we are. David said, "I would have lost heart, unless I had believed that I would see the goodness of the Lord in the land of the living" (Psalm 27:13). His whole character would have changed were it not for his belief in the goodness of God. He would have lost the heart that made him such a valiant warrior and great king.

In the salvation of our soul, the heart is of pivotal importance. Our very faith is initiated in the heart. In his famous passage on salvation, Paul writes, "But what does it say? 'The word is near you, in your mouth and in your heart' (that is, the word of faith which we preach): that if you confess with your mouth the Lord Jesus and believe in your heart that God has raised Him from the dead, you will be saved" (Rom 10:8-9). Obviously, he obviously is not speaking of the physical organ. He is speaking of our innermost being.

Paul is speaking of that inner seat of our being in Romans 5:5 when he writes, "Now hope does not disappoint, because the love of God has been poured out in our hearts by the Holy Spirit who was given to us." He has poured His love into our hearts and the love of God in us creates our love for Him. That is exactly what John is referring to in 1 John 4:19 when he writes. "We love Him because He first loved us."

The love of God and our love for God is the very foundation of our faith. Our relationship with our God is a love relationship. Read these words from Ephesians 3:16-19 several times and let the Lord reveal the depths of this passage. Paul prays, "that He would grant you, according to the riches of His glory, to be strengthened with might through His Spirit in the inner man, that Christ may dwell in your hearts through faith; that you, being rooted and grounded in love, may be able to comprehend with all the saints what is the width and length and depth and height— to know the love of Christ which passes knowledge; that you may be filled with all the fullness of God."

As the reality of Christ dwelling in our heart sinks into our being, we begin to experience the all-encompassing nature of agape love. We begin to love our God with all our heart. To love God with all our heart is to love Him with a total sincerity of our thoughts, emotions, and will. There can be no hypocrisy or compromise in our commitment and compassion.

Love the LORD Your God With All Your Soul

To further express the fullness of this love we are to render to God, Jesus says that we must love the Lord our God with all our heart and all our soul. But what does that mean? Why does the Lord add the soul as a further definition of what is required? The New Testament word translated soul is the Greek word *psyche*. This word carries various shades of meaning that revolve around the immaterial life-force. The English word psychology is the combination of this word *psyche* and the word *logos*. Psychology, then, is the study of the soul. It is not simply the study of the brain. It is the study of the inner qualities of a person that makes them behave as they do. That is why psychology is classified as part of the field of behavioral sciences.

The soul is the life-force of the natural man as surely as the spirit is the life-force of the spiritual man. This life-force is the inner part that is the very life of the person. It is the seat of all passions, emotions, and desires. As such, it is the center of the human personality, self, ego, and individuality. Because the soul is immaterial by nature, it is more difficult to explain what it is than what it does.

As the seat of desires and passions, the soul defines and initiates our hopes, aspirations, and dreams. The soul draws upon all the memories of the past, both good and bad. Therefore, the soul experiences the full gamut of emotions. No wonder the writer of Hebrews warns against the root of bitterness that can spring up in the soul. The experiences of life can cause the soul to experience anger, fear, guilt, loneliness, frustration, emptiness, and helplessness. But the soul also responds in love, joy, hope, satisfaction, contentment, peace, and praise. All these emotions and passions flow from the soul.

David was a man of intense passion. We see this first displayed in his conflict with Goliath. As he listens to his brothers' fears and hears the taunting of Goliath, his passions are stirred. As a matter of fact, the highest point and lowest point in his life are both filled with passion. The story of David and Goliath is the story of intense passion for God and His name. The story of David and Bathsheba is the story of illicit passion for a woman. Is it any wonder that the book of Psalms records the word "soul" more than any other book in the Bible? The word itself is used one hundred times, and the full spectrum of the emotions is expressed even when the actual word is not utilized.

Let us examine just a few of these expressions to help us get an understanding of the depths of expressions of the soul. In Psalm 25:16, David expresses intense loneliness from his troubles. "Turn to me and be gracious to me, for I am lonely and afflicted" (NIV). On the other end of the spectrum, he rejoices over his deliverance from his troubles, in Psalm 40. He writes, "I waited patiently for the LORD; He turned to me and heard my cry. He lifted me out of the slimy pit, out of the mud and mire; He set my feet on a rock and gave me a firm place to stand. He put a new song in my mouth, a hymn of praise to our God. Many will see and fear and put their trust in the LORD."

David expresses in Psalms 31:10 that he experiences sorrow and grief throughout his life. Then in Psalm 4:7, he proclaims that God has "filled his heart with joy and gladness." In Psalm 42:5, he speaks to his own soul, which is filled with discouragement and turmoil. "Why are you downcast, O my soul? Why are you disquieted within me?" Then he instructs his own soul to "hope in God, for I will yet praise Him for the help of His countenance." Two verses later, he expresses the joy of God's presence. "The Lord will command His lovingkindness in the daytime, and in the night His song shall be with me." His experience and memory of that "song in the night" causes him to sing, "As the deer pants for the water brooks, So pants my soul for You, O God My soul thirsts for God, for the living God" (Ps 42:1-2).

Ralph Waldo Emerson expressed the depths of the soul when he wrote, "What lies behind us and what lies before us are tiny matters compared to what lies within us." David expresses that same sentiment in Psalm 103. "Bless the Lord, O my soul; and all that is within me, bless His holy name." In the context of Christ's command to love the Lord with all our heart and soul, we might say, "Love the Lord, O my soul; and all that is within me love His holy name."

Love the LORD Your God With All Your Mind

When the Lord commands us to love God with all our heart and soul, He is addressing the desire, passion, and emotional level of the person. But that is not your "all." He adds to these the intellectual level when He commands that we love God with all our minds as well. Our love for God is an emotional, passionate expression, but it is not an unreasonable expression. It is our intellectual awareness of who God is and what He has done that stirs our emotions and passions.

The mind is an energy that generates the activity of the brain. All thinking, feeling, and determination come from the mind. If we are to love God with the totality of our being, the intellectual part of our being must be engaged. An emotional love is a shallow love, for emotions are based upon feelings that change with the wind. For a relationship to be meaningful, it must involve the intellect as well. In this *agape* type of loving relationship, the mind originates the thoughts and then the heart and soul supply the passion and desire. All three parts work together in harmony so that the being is consumed in the project.

We can divide the mind into basically three distinct but interlocking layers: the conscious, the unconscious, and the subconscious. The Lord commands us to love Him with ALL our mind. So, let's take a moment to examine these three layers of our thought process. Frequently, the image of an iceberg is employed to symbolize the mind. The conscious mind is the visible part of the iceberg; the part that protrudes above the water. We could say that it is the part that touches the outside world.

But as is true with an iceberg, the visible portion is only a small piece of the whole. Much more lies undetected under the surface. The subconscious and unconscious make up the larger portions of the mind. The conscious mind is the home of our sensory knowledge; what we see, hear, smell, touch, etc. The subconscious mind is where all our short-term memories reside. The unconscious mind would be represented by the lowest parts of the iceberg located in the deep, dark depths. That is where all the information of past experiences and learning is stored.

Let me explain how the three parts work together with an illustration from my past. I started preaching and writing decades ago. In those days, there were no personal computers or Bible software. I relied on books for all my research, and I used a typewriter for all my writing. My typewriter and paper would represent the conscious mind. It is there that my thoughts were organized, focused, and made visible by the typewriter. Spread across my desk, you would find a myriad of Bible translations, commentaries, and reference material that were being used as data for what was being typed. The books on my desk would represent the subconscious mind. They were the pieces of information that supplied the immediate information that was being used for the writing. Beyond the books on my desk was my personal library of over one thousand books and a file cabinet of stored resources. My books and files would represent the unconscious resources of the mind. These resources were information that was readily available to draw upon at any time and had supplied the books on my desk.

Remember, Jesus commanded that we love the LORD, our God, with ALL our heart, with ALL our soul, with ALL our mind. All three levels of the mind are to be involved in our love for God. Our beliefs and behaviors are rooted in the unconscious storehouse of our memories and past experiences. Our more recent memories and experiences of the subconscious are drawn upon by the conscious mind to direct our decision-making and focus. The conscious mind is the captain on the bridge, but the real work is done below deck. Again, those words of Psalm 103 counsel us to "forget not all His benefits." As we remember all of our benefits, we will love the Lord with all our mind.

We must examine our thoughts to confirm that we are loving God with all our mind. In 2 Corinthians 13:5, Paul counsels us to examine ourselves continually. Eugene Peterson does an excellent job of interpreting this concept in *The Message*. "Test yourselves to make sure you are solid in the faith. Don't drift along taking everything for granted. Give yourselves regular checkups. You need firsthand evidence, not mere hearsay, that Jesus Christ is in you. Test it out." If you are to love God with all your mind, you must first examine yourself and your experience with Christ. Don't rely upon what others have told you. You need firsthand experience. According to 1 Corinthians 1:9, God has "called you into the fellowship of His Son, Jesus Christ our Lord." We must examine ourselves and confirm that our love is founded upon this fellowship. Once we have confirmed the reality of our love relationship with God, those memories are stored in our mental files. Those memories form the foundation of our Love for God

So, we see that this word, translated as "mind," refers to memories, reflection, meditation, thoughts, and understanding. John has the nickname of the "beloved apostle" or "the apostle that Jesus loved." If Peter is the apostle to the Jews and Paul is the apostle to the Gentiles, John is the apostle of love. In his first letter to the church, he writes, "And we know that the Son of God has come and has given us an understanding, that we may know Him who is true; and we are in Him who is true, in His Son Jesus Christ. This is the true God and eternal life" (1 John 5:20). This word "understanding" is this word "mind." We can have a mind that knows God.

We are to love God to such a degree that our meditation and reflection is on the love of God which has been poured out on us. We are to love Him so much that He invades our very thought life. This is what David is referring to in Psalm 63:6. "When I remember You on my bed, I meditate on You in the night watches." As we remember and meditate upon His promises and our experience with Him, our love becomes a consuming passion.

Love the LORD Your God With All Your Strength

As we consider this greatest of all commandments, we see that Jesus is directing us to love God with the totality of our being. Loving God with our emotions, desires, and intellect is relatively easy to understand. But Jesus adds that we must love God with all our strength as well.

Most often, you will see this explained as loving God with all the strengths of our life. We are to love God with all the things that make us strong — the strengths of our personality and character. But I don't believe that is what Christ is saying, for that flies in the face of Scripture. In his letter to the Corinthians, Paul writes, "My grace is sufficient for you, for my power is made perfect in weakness. Therefore, I will boast all the more gladly about my weaknesses, so that Christ's power may rest on me. That is why, for Christ's sake, I delight in weaknesses, in insults, in hardships, in persecutions, in difficulties. For when I am weak, then I am strong" (2 Cor 12:9-10 NASB).

But Jesus doesn't command us to love God with our strengths (plural). Rather, He says that we must love God with our strength (singular). The word translated strength is basically the same in the original language as it is in our translation. It means power, force, and might. It speaks of forcefulness. The Meriam-Webster dictionary defines strength as the quality or state of being strong: capacity for exertion or endurance, the power to resist force or attack. We are to intentionally, forcefully love God—no matter how we feel.

Remember that Jesus is simply responding with familiar words to the Scribe. He is reminding him of the Shema. In the Hebrew, this command states: "You shall love the LORD your God with all your heart (*leiv*), with all your soul (*nephesh*), and with all your utmost (*me'od*)." Professor of classical rabbinic literature Reuven Kimelman says, "*Me'od* has a double meaning here. First, it means "might," suggesting you must love the Lord with all your strength. Second, it connotes "financial means," suggesting you must love the Lord with all your wealth and possessions."[4] The command is that we must love God with more than simple words and emotions. We must love God with our actions.

In John 14, Jesus connects love with obedience several times. When James instructs the church that without corresponding action, faith has no power, we could accurately say the same about love. Love without accompanying action is dead. We are not to wait until we feel like loving God—we are to forcefully determine to love Him and display that love in our actions.

My father was a man's man. He had been a POW in WWII and learned to keep his emotions in check. Growing up, I have no memory of him ever telling me that he loved me. But there was never a doubt in my mind that he did. He didn't have to say the words, he lived the words.

While in college, I worked for the railroad driving automobiles off trains. It was the perfect job while attending college. The job paid so well that I only needed to work two or three nights a week. One cold winter night, I started out on my thirty-minute drive home after work. About halfway home, my car stalled out and would not start. I called my dad and explained my predicament. I didn't even have to ask for his help, he just said, "I'll be right there." O, I forgot to mention that it was 2:30 in the morning, and he had to get up for work at 5:30. He loved me with all his strength. That was energized, forceful love. That

---

[4] Reuven Kimelman.(n.d.). The Opening of the Shema Prayer Explained. Brandeis.edu.

is the kind of love that Jesus commands. He is not just looking for verbal expression. He expects love in action.

This last addendum to the "love God" command expresses the sentiment of love in action. We are to love God with all our strength and energy. That is exactly what the Greek word translated "strength" in Mark 12:30 literally means — energy, strength, or force. We are to actively, forcefully love God with all our heart, soul, and mind. This is not some passive love. This is active love. A love so deep that it compels us to act.

In his letter to the Church, James informs us that real faith always creates corresponding action. He writes, "If a brother or sister is naked and destitute of daily food, and one of you says to them, 'Depart in peace, be warmed and filled,' but you do not give them the things which are needed for the body, what does it profit?" (James 2:15-16). He goes on to write that faith without works is dead. That is not only true of real faith, it can just as aptly be applied to real love. Love without works is dead. It is not *agape* love if it is not energized, active love.

PUTTING IT ALL TOGETHER

We are to have a personal love relationship with our God. He has set His hand upon us and we are His people. The prophet Jeremiah spoke of this relationship. "I will give them a heart to know Me, that I am the Lord; and they shall be My people, and I will be their God, for they shall return to Me with their whole heart" (Jer 24:7). The God of all creation, the God who was, and is, and is to come, is our God. And we are to love our God with the totality of our being. We are to love Him energetically with all our emotions and desire. But this is not simply to be some fragile emotion of love. We are to love Him willfully, taking time to reflect upon the grandeur of his goodness.

We are to utilize the full capacity of our intelligence in loving Him. The more we know Him, the more deeply we love Him. Paul said that he is "persuaded that neither death nor life, nor angels nor principalities nor powers, nor things present nor things to come, nor height nor depth, nor any other created thing, shall be able to separate us from the love of God" (Rom 8:38-39). This love is so all-encompassing that nothing can stop it. This is the Greatest Commandment, the command of the New Covenant. Love God with the essence of your being.

How do I love thee? Let me count the ways.
I love thee to the depth and breadth and height
My soul can reach, when feeling out of sight
For the ends of being and ideal grace.

Elizabeth Barret Browning
How Do I Love Thee, Sonnet 43

4

LOVE YOUR NEIGHBOR

Do not waste time bothering whether you 'love' your
neighbor; act as if you did. As soon as we do this we find
one of the great secrets. When you are behaving as if you
loved someone, you will presently come to love him.
—C. S. Lewis

In the last chapter, we examined Jesus' response to the scribe's question about which of the commandments was the greatest. The Jewish *Book of Commandments* contains over six hundred commands. The commands are divided into positive commands and negative commands. In Mark 12, we find a scribe voicing a current lawyers' debate over which type of command was the greatest; the positive, "Thou Shall," commands or the negative, "Thou shall not," commands.

In answering the question, Jesus quotes a proclamation with which the scholar would be deeply familiar. Jesus' answer is the simple recitation of the *Shema.* "Hear, O Israel: The Lord our God, the Lord is one! You shall love the Lord your God with all your heart, with all your soul, with all your mind, and with all your strength." This proclamation is the central affirmation of the Jews. In a world of polytheism, they are monotheistic. Their God is One God and, as such, is deserving of their undying, all-encompassing love. Every faithful Jew proclaimed the *Shema* twice daily: first thing in the morning and last thing in the evening. The scribe had spoken those words thousands of times. You can almost imagine him nodding his head as he recites the words along with Jesus.

But then, Jesus adds a second command. This command is also a positive command. "And the second, like it, is this: 'You shall love your neighbor as yourself" (Mark 12:31). To assure that the young lawyer understood His answer, He adds, "There is no other commandment greater than these." Since both commands are positive, Jesus is answering that the positive commands are the greatest. The requirements of the Law are met by fulfilling these two positive commands.

If we love God with all our being and love our neighbors with the same love with which we love ourselves, we need not worry about the negative commands. As a matter of fact, Matthew records a phrase not listed in Mark's account. Matthew 22:40 states, "On these two commandments hang all the Law and the Prophets." If the young lawyer could fulfill these two simple commands in fullness, he would satisfy the other 611 commands of the *mitzvah* without even thinking about it.

Notice that Jesus says that the second commandment is like the first. We are to love God with the whole of our life—heart, soul, mind, and strength. In like manner, we are to love others with the totality of our self. We are to love our neighbor with all our heart, soul, mind, and strength. These two summary laws display the fact that if we obey what He tells us, we will not get involved in the things we shouldn't.

Since all the Law and the Prophets hang on these two commands, it seems fitting that we must look closely at both. In the last chapter, we spent time examining the command to love the LORD, our God, with all our being. Now, let us turn our attention to this second commandment and examine it closely.

On the surface, the command seems so simple. Love your neighbor. But as is true of most of Jesus' words, there is an underlying message that must be uncovered.

So, exactly what did Christ mean when He commanded us to love our neighbor as ourselves?

WHAT TYPE OF LOVE?

In Chapter Two, we examined the Greek words used to delineate the three main types of love. If you remember, *phileo* means to have ardent affection and feelings for someone. It is an emotionally based and impulsive type of love. At its core, *phileo* is simply a natural human affection with its powerful feelings and sentiments. With that in mind, it would seem appropriate to expect Jesus to use the word for natural affection here.

When Jesus speaks of loving your neighbor, it would be in perfect context and usage for Him to have used the word, *phileo,* which is often interpreted as brotherly love. But that is not what He says. He uses the highest word—the same word He used in the preceding verse about loving God. He uses the word *agape.* We are to love others with that all-encompassing, selfless love. He goes far beyond the scope of natural affection for our neighbors. He is telling us to love our neighbors with the same high love with which we are to love God. We are to love our neighbors with the same love that put Jesus on the cross: wholehearted, selfless love.

In his love letter to the church, John reinforces this connection between loving God and loving people. He writes, "If someone says, 'I love God,' and hates his brother, he is a liar; for he who does not love his brother whom he has seen, how can he love God whom he has not seen?" (I John 4:20). If you really love God, the Creator of all that is, then you will also love His creation. Man is made in the direct image of God. If we say we love God, we should also love His image. If we cannot love His image, we are not loving God with the totality of our being. Jesus' command is straightforward and perfectly clear. We are to love our neighbors with the same love with which we love Him.

It is easy to say that we love God. But if we scrutinize our heart and actions carefully, we usually find imperfections in that love. It is difficult to truly love God purely and perfectly—with all our heart, soul, mind, and strength. But it is extremely more difficult to love our neighbors with that same purity and passion. Our neighbors do not always behave like God. Their actions are not always lovely. They are often self-absorbed and rude. The things they say to us and about us are not always kind. Unlike our loving God, their desire is not always to bless us. Sometimes they act rather poorly.

Yet, He wants us to love those who are unlovely with the same love that we have for the Lover of all. He wants us to love the homeless and the thief with the same love with which we love our Father God. We are to love those who take advantage of us with the same love with which we love our Savior, who went to the cross for us.

He even expects us to love those who have wounded us. The pain of those emotional wounds scars our soul. Many of the deepest scars come not from our enemies, but from our friends. Some of our deepest wounds are inflicted by those we love the most. Most of us can identify with the prophet, Zechariah, when he was questioned about the scars on his back. He responded those were the wounds he received in the house of his friends.

No one understood the depths of those wounds more than Jesus. The shouts of "Hosanna!" as He entered Jerusalem had turned to "Crucify Him!" by Friday. His chosen few would deny they even know Him. One of the twelve would betray Him with a kiss. In John 15:13, Jesus says, "Greater love has no one than this, than to lay down one's life for his friends." Then He tells the disciples that He no longer calls them servants. He now calls them His friends. Even while making this proclamation, He is well aware that they will abandon Him and deny even knowing Him. He will experience deep wounds in the house of these friends. And yet, He willfully lays down His life for them. The prophet Isaiah spoke of Jesus being wounded for our transgressions. Yet, He proclaimed, "Father forgive them. They don't understand what they are doing."

In reality, He had already laid down His life for them. He was the creative force in all of creation. Yet, He loved us so much that

70

4 Love Your Neighbor

He left His home in glory to experience the trials and tribulations of life on earth. In Philippians 2, Paul tells us that Christ made Himself of "no reputation" and became an obedient servant. Jesus laid down His life for us by taking on the limitations of human existence. He was the creative force of all creation and dwelt in the eternal Oneness of the Godhead. He left the limitless perfection of that existence to take on the finiteness of humanity. The creator of all things became part of the creation.

When we think of laying down our life for our friends, we immediately tend to think of dying for others as Jesus did for us. But He is not commanding us to die for our friends, He is commanding that we live for them. We are to give our life in serving others with the love of Christ.

In the Garden, Jesus prayed, "Not My will, but Thy will" (Luke 22:42). Not only is that a perfect picture of submission, but it is also a picture of all-encompassing, self-sacrificing love. If we love our neighbor with this highest of loves, we will echo Christ's words. "This is not about what I want, but what you want. This is not about what makes me happy—it is about what pleases you. It is not what I want to do—it is about what you want me to do." Getting to that place of putting the desires of others before our own will require true humility flowing out of *agape* love.

This *agape* love that He is addressing causes us to lay down our very life, our deepest desires, for the benefit of others. This is the purest kind of love—the love that asks nothing in return. In the great hymn of love, 1 Corinthians 13, Paul is speaking of this love when he writes that love does not seek its own will. Loving others as yourself is not about trying to convince them to agree with you. It is about loving people, whether you agree with their lifestyle or not. Sometimes we get so focused on other people's sins that we fail to love with the selfless love Jesus commanded.

We tend to judge the sins of others harshly. Especially those sins with which we are not personally entangled. We tend to consider those sins worse than the sin in our own life. If we fudge a little bit on the income tax, that sin is not as bad as the guy who is cheating on his wife. But cheating is cheating, and stealing is stealing. Even if the stealing is just taking a pencil from a fellow worker's desk. The worst sin is always the sin we see in others when we are not actively committing that grievance. It is so easy to condemn the conduct of others and downplay the sin in our own lives.

In Matthew 7, Jesus commands us to "judge not." He is not saying to not make judgments about right or wrong. He is commanding that we not be judgmental. We must make judgments about right and wrong, but we cannot know the motive or the heart of the person. We are to judge the action without judging the person. Judgmentalism is an act of pride and God hates pride.

In this passage in Matthew, Jesus asks why we try to remove a speck of dust from our neighbor's eye when we have a log of pride in our own eye. He is saying that we are not to judge our neighbor; we are to love our neighbor. If we see our neighbor in sin, we are to pray for him rather than condemn him. And we are to love our neighbors as Christ loves us—love without conditions or compromise.

Years ago, the Lord used Chuck Girard's song, "Don't Shoot the Wounded" to break my pride in this area. I was listening to the song while driving, and suddenly, the Lord convicted me so clearly that I had to stop on the side of the road and repent. The stanza that the Lord used to speak to me is as follows:

Myself I've been forgiven for so many awful things
I've been cleansed and washed and bathed so many times
That when I see a brother who has fallen from the way
I just can't find the license to convict him of his crimes
So, I say...
Don't shoot the wounded, they need us more than ever
They need our love no matter what it is they've done
Sometimes we just condemn them,
And don't take time to hear their story
Don't shoot the wounded, someday you might be one

We are often quick to pick up rocks to stone the sinner. Yet, we have been convicted, forgiven, and cleansed of so many evil things ourselves. What hypocrites we are! We can tolerate our own sin, but we have issues with the sins someone else commits. Our sole responsibility and calling is not to condemn but to love.

People need love in a relationship much more than they need correction. People are waiting for the Church to love them. They are waiting for us to really care about them. The problem is that many times the Church cares more about issues than about people. We forget that people are what's really important, not the minor issues at hand.

Jesus once illustrated this kind of love as He dined with a prominent Pharisee. He pointed out that we should not vie for prominent seats of honor, but rather take a low seat and let the host elevate us. Then he explained what unselfish, nonreciprocal love might look like in a practical life situation:

We find His illustration in Luke 14:12-14. "Then He also said to him who invited Him, 'When you give a dinner or a supper, do not ask your friends, your brothers, your relatives, nor rich neighbors, lest they also invite you back, and you be repaid. But when you give a feast, invite the poor, the maimed, the lame, the blind. And you will be blessed, because they cannot repay you; for you shall be repaid at the resurrection of the just.'"

Let's be honest. Few of us operate with this kind of unselfish concern for others. Most of us do not go to lunch trying to find someone to invite that we do not know or someone in need that we could bless. Jesus is saying that if we love like He loves, we will dine with those who can never reciprocate the gesture. Blessings will then begin to flow because we will be operating in this perfect love that He has commanded. Jesus fed thousands of people who heard Him preach because of the compassion He had for them. His only motivation for feeding the thousands was His love for the people and His desire to express that love.

Jesus continually lived out this kind of love that He commands. The amazing thing about Jesus was that He was a rabbi, and in the Jewish culture, a rabbi was virtually untouchable. Yet, Jesus was extremely touchable and available for all people. You remember the story of the woman with issue of blood that was healed when she touched the hem of His robe. Jesus turned and asked, "Who touched me?" Peter reacted in astonishment at Jesus' question. He said, "What do you mean who touched you? Look at the crowd pressing in upon us. Hundreds of people have touched you. You are always within the reach of the people." Jesus was like the politician who steps beyond his bodyguards and goes into the midst of the crowd. Jesus' love and care for the people forced him out of the confines of rules and expectations. He stayed among the people and habitually violated social etiquette. Every time He touched a leper, He broke the law.

It was against the law to touch lepers in Jesus' day. By Law, the lepers were to stay outside of town and proclaim themselves unclean if anyone approached. The same was true of anyone with an open sore or exposed wound. When the woman with the issue of blood touched the hem of His garment, she took an enormous risk. By Law, she was to declare herself unclean when people even moved close to her. But she was desperate and squeezed her way through the crowd just to touch His garment. Her need for love was greater than her risk of punishment for breaking the Law.

Jesus was always accessible to those who needed His love the most. When He washed the disciples' feet before the Last Supper, He even washed Judas' feet. He was fully aware of the fact that Judas was going to turn Him over to the authorities and initiate His death. But He loved him anyway. At that last meal with His closest followers, the disciples asked Jesus who would betray Him. He responded, "It is he to whom I shall give a piece of bread when I have dipped it" (John 13:26). As Jesus dipped the bread in the spiced olive oil, He handed it to Judas.

That simple act tells us that Judas was in a place of honor at the Last Supper, seated next to Jesus on His left. John was positioned on Jesus' right in the ultimate place of honor. We know this because John leaned his head on Jesus' shoulder as they reclined at the low table, resting on their left elbow. From this position, He would need to learn his head back towards Jesus to speak with Him. That means that Judas must have been on Jesus' left.

I have often thought about the words of Jesus when Judas betrayed Him. He tells Judas, "Will you betray Me with a kiss?" So many times, that phrase is portrayed harshly or sarcastically in a rebuke. From what I see in the life of Jesus and His dealings with Judas, I don't think that is a correct interpretation. I think Christ's question is a very soft word of disappointed love. I imagine there were tears in His eyes as He looked upon His betrayer.

Obviously, the greatest illustration of *agape* love is when Jesus died for our sins. He displayed the love that says, "I choose to willfully love you, no matter what you have done to me. No matter how badly you hurt me, I will love you. You cannot make me not love you. There is nothing so unlovely that you could do that would cause me not to love you." When He asked forgiveness for those crucifying Him, He displayed the epitome of love. It was this same love that drew people to Him during His ministry on earth. When we begin to live out that kind of love, we will see people desiring what we have.

YOUR NEIGHBOR

On a separate occasion, another scribe tested Jesus with a question about how to gain eternal life. He asked, "Teacher, what shall I do to inherit eternal life?" As is so often the case, Jesus answered the question with a question rather than giving a direct answer.

Jesus asked, "What is written in the law? What is your reading of it?" In other words, how do you interpret what the Law says?

The lawyer responds with the same answer Jesus gave in Mark 10. "You shall love the Lord your God with all your heart, with all your soul, with all your strength, and with all your mind,' and 'your neighbor as yourself" (Lk 10:27).

Jesus then complimented him on his answer and advised him that if he could fulfill this requirement, he would live. The conversation obviously did not work the way the lawyer anticipated. He was expecting an attack on the Law, not a confirmation of it. So, in a further attempt to trap Jesus, he asks, "If I am to love my neighbor, in your opinion, who is my neighbor?"

What the lawyer did not think about is that it is impossible to trap someone who knows your thoughts. Without hesitation Jesus launched into a story about a Jewish man who was traveling from Jerusalem to Jericho. That is about an eight-hour journey on foot; about fifteen kilometers. Along the way, this man was robbed. Not only did they steal his money, but they also beat him fiercely and even stole his clothing. Near death, he lay there on the side of the road, bleeding and naked.

The road connecting Jericho and Jerusalem was a well-traveled road. As the man lay there, half-dead, a member of the Jewish priesthood came down the road. When the priest saw the man, he simply moved to the other side of the road so as not to be forced to look at the man. After all, if the man happened to die while the priest tended his wounds, the priest would be declared "unclean." So he thought it best to not take the chance. Shortly thereafter, a Levite came along and took the same exact approach. He, too, passed by on the other side of the road.

One can only imagine the hopeless feelings the wounded man must have felt. Finally, a man from Samaria came upon the man. But rather than simply passing by, he stopped and treated the man's wounds. Then, he sat the wounded man upon his own animal and led him to the nearest inn. He cared for the wounded man for the rest of that day. His schedule demanded that he leave the next morning. But rather than just leave the wounded man alone, he gave the innkeeper two days' wages and asked him to attend to the man. He even told the innkeeper that he would cover any additional expenses on his next visit.

After telling the story, Jesus asked the lawyer, "So of these travelers, which of these do you think acted as a neighbor?" Keep in mind that the Samaritans were despised by the Jews, who considered them a mixed race. There was a universal hatred between the two peoples. Even though the answer was obvious, it must have been difficult for this Jewish leader to admit. But swallowing his pride and bigotry, he answered, "Obviously, the one who showed mercy upon the wounded man."

Jesus replied, "There is the answer to your question. Your neighbor is anyone that you see who is in need. Their nationality, tribe, or people group does not matter – they are your neighbor. Now, go and apply this to your own life."

As you think about this story, keep in mind that a priest or a Levite could not touch a corpse without becoming unclean. So, they quite possibly assumed that this man was dead or that he might die in their arms. Instead of checking on him to confirm, they simply passed by on the other side. For these men, the risk of breaking the Law was greater than the reward of showing compassion and love.

There is a great principle to be seen here—the Law is overruled by love. They were more concerned about keeping the Law than meeting the needs of this man. How often do the actions of our own life resemble their response? Sometimes we are more concerned about being right and holy than we are about meeting the needs of those around us. We are more concerned about our own convenience and comfort than about the needs of the one who is hurting.

We can learn many things from the parable of the good Samaritan. The most obvious lesson is that religion does not produce this kind of love. Only a relationship with Jesus will birth this love within you. This kind of love requires you to give of yourself and your resources. Most of us are much more comfortable giving our resources than ourselves. We will give money if someone else will take care of the situation. Many times, we, too, want to pass by on the other side rather than deal with the hurting person. Yet, the God of love gave of Himself and became a lowly human because He loved us. He suffered a human death because of His love for us. We have been given so much love—how can we not give of ourselves to show that same love to others?

Several years ago, one of the ladies in my church went to Venezuela on a mission trip. During that trip, most of the people were involved in what appeared to be spiritual things like teaching and witnessing. She felt like she did not have anything to offer. However, there was a young man who was so hopeless and helpless that he could not care for himself. For one week, this woman lived for that boy. She cleaned him, bathed him, fed him, and gave him love. On the Day of Judgment, the highest rewards from that trip will not likely go to those involved in public ministry. . . but to she who loved. Her actions were not a big thing. They were not the out-front visible tasks, but what she did was the loving thing.

The story of the good Samaritan reveals to us that your neighbor is anyone in need. Often, we must look beyond our physical neighborhoods to find our neighbors, and sometimes we only need to look next door. Brother Leonard Ravenhill once gave me this little nugget of truth. "Sometimes the poorest people live in the richest houses." The term "poor" can be used to describe many different situations. Many times, it has nothing to do with money. There are people in our world who are in poverty of a simple human touch. In our isolated modern societies, people are starving for the human touch. People that you interact with daily may go for months without being touched by another human.

The wounded walk among us, and as the poet says, "There is none so blind as he who will not see." If we are to ever love others as ourselves, much less love our neighbor as Christ loves us, we must open our eyes and see. We must learn to see the wounded lying along life's road. They are all around us. We simply fail to see. Keith Green speaks as one of the prophets of old in his song "Asleep in the Light." Although decades old now, the words still pierce the heart.

Do you see? Do you see?

All the people sinking down?
Don't you care? Don't you care?
Are you gonna let them drown?
How can you be so numb?
Not to care if they come
You close your eyes and pretend the job's done
"Oh, bless me, Lord! Bless me, Lord!"
You know, it's all I ever hear
No one aches, no one hurts.
No one even sheds one tear.
But He cries, He weeps, He bleeds,
And He cares for your needs.
And you just lay back and keep soaking it in

We are here on this blue orb to express God's love to a lost and dying world. We must open our eyes and see the hopeless, helpless condition of this self-centered generation. I once heard it said that every generation of believers is responsible for that generation of lost. What a humbling and terrifying thought. We will one day stand before the Judgment Seat of Christ and give an account of the hurting people of our generation. We will experience the awesome, awful presence of pure love as we stand before Him, beholding His pierced hands and feet. In order to experience His love flowing through us, we need to learn how to truly abide in the Vine.

AS YOURSELF

I often hear it taught that we must learn to love ourselves before we can love others. While this may sound good from a psychological perspective, there is no Scriptural foundation for this counsel. Those who support this counsel tend to cite the very passage we are examining. "You shall love your neighbor as yourself." They believe loving yourself is a prerequisite to loving others. In their position, if you don't love yourself, you will not be able to love others. So, you must first learn to love yourself. This idea puts self at the forefront.

If that is true, why would Paul warn in 2 Timothy 3 that in these last days, men would be lovers of themselves? He wasn't saying that in a complimentary fashion. He said that the last days would be "perilous times." If loving self is mandatory to loving others, these men would have a great capacity to love others. Obviously, that was not Paul's intent, nor Christ's intent in His command.

As a matter of fact, Jesus' call is quite the opposite. "He said to them all, 'If anyone desires to come after Me, let him deny himself, and take up his cross daily, and follow Me'" (Luke 9:23). You are not commanded to love yourself. You are commanded to "die" to Self and its selfish interests. In reality, His teachings make it clear that we are not even to be thinking about our "self." When you are giving yourself to other people, the thought of loving yourself never enters your mind. This principle is evident in marriage. If you are to have a truly successful marriage, you must live to serve your spouse. The pleasure of your life is found in pleasing the other person. When I live my life to serve my wife, my own thoughts and needs do not enter into the equation. My needs are met in my serving her. Ideally, she lives her life to serve me. But that is not a prerequisite to my loving her. Disputes cease when you are living to serve the other person. We must deny self—die to self—and get self out of the way in order to fully love others.

As we die to self and live for others, we suddenly understand contentment and fulfillment. We are secure in His love. There is no place in Scripture where we are told to love ourselves. In 1 John 4, John explains the principle that God is love and when we abide in Him, we are living in love. Because of His great love for us—a love so great that Christ died for us—we know love. We are secure in ourselves. God, the creator of all that exists, loves us.

Because God loves us and fills us with His love, we love Him. We love others because His love flows out of us. We are told to love God and love others—He will take care of loving us. Jesus addresses this in Matthew 6 when He tells us not to worry about what we will wear or eat or the basic needs of life - God will take care of us. Jesus commands His followers to seek the kingdom of God and His righteousness, and everything else will fall into place.

To make certain His followers clearly understood what He was commanding, He clarified the love He expects in His final instructions to the twelve. He is very specific about this *agape* love that He expects us to have for our neighbor. This expectation goes far beyond loving others as we love ourselves. We must love with the same depth of love that He has for us. "This is My commandment, that you love one another as I have loved you" (Jn 15:12). That takes loving our neighbor to a whole new level. Loving our neighbor as our self is a deep kind of love. But loving others as He loved us is a totally different dimension of love. He loved us so much that He laid down His life for us. In His death, He exhibited this *agape* love that takes no thought for self-interests.

John gives us a wonderful revelation of this love in his first letter to the church. In 1 John 4:8, he reminds us that God is love. He goes on to explain, "In this, the love of God was manifested toward us, that God has sent His only begotten Son into the world, that we might live through Him." Here we find the secret to loving others. God is love. If God lives in us, love lives in us. In John 15, Christ says that He is the vine, and we are the branches. If we abide in Him, we produce His fruit. In Galatians 5, we find the list of that fruit. As Paul lists the fruit, the first fruit listed is love. As we abide in Christ, we are filled with His love and produce love.

According to 1 John 4:10, because God loves us, we can love others. "In this is love, not that we loved God, but that He loved us and sent His Son to be the propitiation for our sins. Beloved, if God so loved us, we also ought to love one another." When one falls in love, everything is lovely to that person. There is no thought of selfish interests. Love makes everything lovely. When you abide in Love, you will naturally love others as Christ loves you. We are to follow in His footsteps and live to serve rather than living to be served.

The more you focus on yourself, the more dissatisfied you become. On the other hand, great satisfaction and contentment come when we rest in the love of God, oblivious to the shortcomings and frailty of self. When we focus on the Lord and on others, that peace that surpasses explanation settles into us. We know we are secure in His love. Nothing can separate us from this great love. This inner security allows us to love others as Christ loves us

IMPORTANCE OF LOVING OTHERS

As much as the Bible does not emphasize loving ourself, it does emphasize loving others. The apostle John is known as the Beloved Apostle. In his first epistle, he speaks seriously about loving others: "For this is the message that you heard from the beginning, that we should love one another" (I John 3:11). In the 4th chapter, he tells us that our love for others proves we know God. He goes so far as to say that anyone who does not love others does not know God.

Love is the principal topic of all the New Testament writings. Jesus says, "By this all will know that you are My disciples, if you have love for one another" (John 13:35). Isn't it amazing that He doesn't say that we will be known for our doctrine or buildings or exciting worship? If we are truly His disciples, we will love others. We will be recognized as followers of Jesus by the love that pours out of us. In his famous hymn of praise for love, Paul said, "And now abide faith, hope, love, these three; but the greatest of these is love" (1 Cor 13:13). Our faith works through our love, and our hope is founded upon love. How often we fail to make love first and foremost.

Paul begins that famous chapter, reminding us of the importance of love. Under the influence of the Holy Spirit, he writes, "Though I speak with the tongues of men and of angels, but have not love, I have become sounding brass or a clanging cymbal. And though I have the gift of prophecy, and understand all mysteries and all knowledge, and though I have all faith, so that I could remove mountains, but have not love, I am nothing. And though I bestow all my goods to feed the poor, and though I give my body to be burned, but have not love, it profits me nothing" (1Cor 13:1-3).

Take a moment to meditate upon what he is saying. The gifts of the Spirit are useless without love. Having great understanding and knowledge does not benefit the church without love. We spend much time teaching and preaching on faith. But Paul goes so far as to say that even if you have faith to move mountains, without love you are nothing. Even if you make great sacrifice, it profits you nothing without love.

We tend to think that the New Testament church reached the world by great preaching accompanied by signs and wonders. Over and over, we have tried to imitate that pattern. But the early church won people to Jesus by loving them. The miracles flowed out of that love. If we become miracle-conscious without becoming love-conscious, we have misunderstood the miraculous power of God's love. The miracles follow the love. When you learn to love as God loves, you will do the miraculous as Jesus did.

Over and over, the gospels portray Jesus as being moved with compassion. Galatians 5:6 tells us that faith works through love. It is love that fuels the faith. Love stimulates us to bring things to bear. Jesus was moved with compassion to heal the sick. It was not because He wanted to display His great power and miracle-working ability. He was moved with compassion for the sick and dying individuals around Him. When we get honest with ourselves, we often realize that our motives are not totally pure. The desire is more selfish and self-seeking than based upon love. Most of us want to perform miracles to justify our position. How often do we see people fall into pride over the performance of those miracles?

The compassion and love of God that indwells us should push us towards miracles so that the hurting can be healed. During a trip to Poland in 1990, God moved mightily in the outpouring of healings. We were seeing God do phenomenal things on the streets of Katowice. Blind people gained their sight instantly. Wheelchairs were evacuated. All sorts of miracles were occurring. One day as we were concluding the outdoor meeting, a woman pushed a wheelchair in front of me. The little girl in that wheelchair was about the same age as my daughter back home. I felt my heart fill with love for that little girl and my expectations grew high. As I knelt in front of the wheelchair and placed my hands upon her feet, I understood what it meant to be moved with compassion.

I do not know if I have ever known the kind of heartsick pain that I felt that day when that little girl did not get healed instantly. I had seen God do so many wonderful things that day. I do not know why she left still bound to that chair except that my faith working through my love was not sufficient to move this mountain. As I looked into the eyes of that mother, I saw the pain and disappointment. In spite of the language barrier between us, I personally felt her pain. The memory of that event still plagues me, and it is why I speak so much about healing. Seeing that mother's look of disappointment when nothing happened instantly broke me. I could not even give her the good charismatic saying, "Believe God, and in two or three days, it will happen." All I could do was just walk away with a new understanding of compassion.

God's desire is that we walk in the compassion and love that I felt in Poland that day. But not just compassion and love for healing. Compassion and love for the lost state of their soul. What would happen to the world today if the church decided to love people as Christ loved? What if we chose to love those who agreed with us as well as those who disagreed with us?

In 1 John 3:15, John goes so far as to write that he who hates his brother does not have eternal life. He is stating that you cannot truthfully call yourself a follower of Jesus if hate resides in your heart instead of love. If you say that you hate someone, you need to be careful. It is contrary to who you are. He is not saying that if you hate, you lose your salvation. Rather, He says that if you can hold that hatred, it proves that your old nature has not died. John reminds us of this a few verses later in 1 John 4:20. "If someone says, 'I love God,' and hates his brother, he is a liar; for he who does not love his brother whom he has seen, how can he love God whom he has not seen?" He is not addressing the love you feel for your biological brother. He is talking about the men and women around you in everyday life. If I love God, I will love people, for He loves people. He doesn't just love those who receive Him. He loves the entire world.

When we speak ill of other Christians, we are talking about the bride of Christ. If you want to anger a young man, start talking badly about his bride. That is the quickest way to find yourself in a conflict. Likewise, when we talk about churches having trouble, we should do it with a broken heart because that is Christ's bride.

John reminds us in 1 John 3:18, "My little children, let us not love in word or in tongue, but in deed and in truth." My father was never much for telling me that he loved me. I never remember him coming to me and saying, "I just want you to know that I love you." But there was never a single doubt in my mind that he loved me. He continually displayed it to me. If my car broke down in the middle of nowhere in the middle of the night, I never questioned whether I could call my dad. He was always there. Words are powerless without action. So do not simply talk about love—show it!

Jesus emphasized the importance of loving others in His story of the sheep and the goats found in Matthew 25:31-46. He goes so far as to say that when you actively love others, you are loving Him. Here He tells us that when He returns in glory, He will set the sheep on His right hand and the goats on the left. The sheep are symbolic of those who follow Him. He will say to the sheep, "Come, you blessed of My Father, inherit the kingdom prepared for you from the foundation of the world: for I was hungry and you gave Me food; I was thirsty and you gave Me drink; I was a stranger and you took Me in; I was naked and you clothed Me; I was sick and you visited Me; I was in prison and you came to Me" (v. 34-36).

This explanation will be confusing to the righteous sheep. They will explain that they don't remember ever seeing Him in those needy conditions. Jesus then tells them that as often as they showed love to others, they expressed their love for Him. The opposite will be true of the goats on His left. As often as they passed over the needs of others, they passed Him.

There is more to righteousness than just what Jesus did for us on the cross. Loving others is putting action to the righteousness that He has given us. He gave us the right-standing at the right hand of the throne. Now, we are expected to walk in the right-wayness. 1 John 3:7 tells us he who practices righteousness is righteous. He is not saying that the practice of righteousness makes you righteous. He is saying that if you are righteous, you will walk in the right way. If you really love God, you will love others.

As we love others, we are expressing our love for their Creator. We are reciprocating the love that we have received from God. If we do not love others, it is evident that we have not really been touched by His love. I have spent many years traveling around the world, teaching the truths of the Gospel. Yet, the thing that people remember most from the visits are the hugs and expressions of love. People are waiting for you to put your arm around them and say, "I love you."

As you have done it to one of the least of these My brethren,
you did it unto Me.
-- Jesus

5
RECONCILIATION

God did not wait for a change of heart on our part. He made the first move. Indeed, He did more than that. He did all that was necessary to secure our reconciliation, including our change of heart. Even though He is the One offended by our sin, He is the One who makes amends to Himself through the death of Christ.
— Jerry Bridges

Man was created to have fellowship with God, but man's choice caused an offense to that fellowship. In the Garden of Eden, man had perfect fellowship with God—for a period of time. We do not know how long the perfect relationship lasted. We tend to think that Adam and Eve were created one day, and the next day they fell into sin. For all we know, there could have been one hundred years between those events. The concept of time is a little different in the Hebrew language, and we are not told how much time passed before they committed the original sin. We do know that they lived in close communion with the Father, and then one day, they made that fatal error.

THE BREACH

Man's fatal error was his determination to taste evil. The allurement of the fullness of knowledge, or at least what he thought was the fullness, was too great a temptation. We often wonder why God became so upset with Adam and Eve for simply eating that fruit. But the issue was not the eating of the fruit. The issue was their unbelief in God's word that the knowledge of evil would kill them. When they gave in to temptation, they tasted evil for the first time.

God is completely pure—no spot or blemish can be found in Him. Man was created in His perfect image with no knowledge of evil. Once man tasted evil, he fell from the spiritual plane of the perfect God. Thus, it became impossible for the God-intended fellowship to exist. Their unbelief violated the fellowship and initiated the breach. That breach has been passed down to every living soul that followed.

We are born into this world with the sinful nature of unbelief that we inherited from Adam. Romans 5:19 says, "For as by one man's disobedience many were made sinners, so also by one Man's obedience many will be made righteous." That is what Paul is referring to in 1 Corinthians 15:22 when he writes, "In Adam, all die." Due to the sinful nature that we inherited from our father, Adam, we are born in sin. That sin separates us from the glorious life God intended. That sinful nature is what Paul is speaking of in Ephesians 2:1 when he says that we "were dead in our trespasses and sins." Adam and Eve violated our fellowship with God in the Garden, and we have continued that breach by our own choices. We have fallen from the glorious relationship God intended. "For all have sinned and fallen short of the glory of God" (Rom 3:23). We were the glorious creation, created in His image to reflect His glory to all of creation. We were His imagers in this three-dimensional world.

The serpent told Eve that if she ate of that fruit, she would be like God. When the serpent made that claim, he was speaking a double lie. First, Adam and Eve were already like God. Second, when they ate of the fruit, they became unlike God. This is exactly how the devil operates. Jesus even referred to him as the "Father of Lies" (John 8:44). Anytime the demonic whispers in your ear, you can be assured what you are hearing is a liar. Satan is a habitual liar, and he lied to Eve. He says, "You'll be like God," but she was already like God. The moment she ate of the tree, she became unlike God because God does not personally know evil. This evil that Adam and Eve tasted was totally foreign to God's holiness. There can be no evil in perfect holiness. In the first chapter of his letter to the church, James assures us of that fact. He writes, "God cannot be tempted by evil, nor does He tempt anyone with evil." Evil is utterly foreign to His absolute holiness.

Jesus' struggle in the Garden of Gethsemane was not about the physical pain that He knew He was about to endure. When He prayed, "If there is any other way, let this cup pass from me," He was addressing the issue of sin. He had no personal understanding of sin. He had seen sin and experienced people involved in sin, but He had never personally experienced evil in His very being. Now, He was about to dip this cup into the evil of all time and partake of sin. All the sin of every human that had ever lived and ever would live came flooding into Jesus. As He thought about these things here in the Garden, He was in deep turmoil. Luke reports that He actually sweat drops of blood. He had come to earth to remove the breach and restore man's relationship with God. Now, He would pay the price of the reconciliation.

From the very moment of Adam's offense, God has been working to reconcile man back to Himself. In reality, the reconciliation process was put in place long before Adam's offense. According to Revelation 13:8, Christ was crucified before the foundations of the world were laid. That fact is hard for us to comprehend. Some have even said that Christ's death on the cross was the entire purpose of creation. The issue we are addressing here is the conflict between conceptual language and technical language. We live in a technological age. Our world speaks the language of technology. We understand time from a technical perspective.

Consider the fact of God's omniscience. He is all-knowing. He knows the future and the past—He knows everything. If you look at the story of the tower of Babel, we discover an interesting phrase. Genesis 11:5 says that God came down to see the city. If in His omniscience, He already knew what was happening, why did He need to go down and see? Here is the dilemma—our technical mindset is trying to understand a conceptual message.

When we put our technical interpretation on the Bible's conceptual ideas, we find some incongruences. The Bible is not written technically. None of us would be excited about a technical love letter from a love interest that spends three pages explaining love. A love letter is conceptual. It expresses the concept of love, not the details of where it came from or where it is going.

Many fall prey to the idea that God did not know what was going to happen in the Garden. It is as though God created Adam and Eve and was shocked when they failed to believe Him. Many go to the other extreme and say that He planned it all. With that mindset, one falls into predestination and fatalism, which makes man little more than a puppet. In the first vein of thought, God created Adam and Eve, and that experiment was a failure. Then He sent Moses with the Law, and that turned into an even worse failure. So, He finally decided to send Jesus.

While that thinking is not correct, it is not entirely wrong either. We are still trying to deal with the event technically as opposed to dealing with it conceptually. If we think conceptually, we realize the Bible is a book about God and His desired fellowship with man. As such, the concept being presented is one of love and reconciliation. Unlike all other gods, God's glory is His goodness and love. God loves us. Our sin creates the offense that separates us from fellowship with Him. So, God solved that breach and reconciled us back to Himself.

ATONEMENT

Hebrews 11 makes it clear that men of the Old Testament were saved by faith, just as those of the new covenant. When a Jewish man made a sacrifice of a lamb on the Day of Atonement, he was looking forward to Calvary. One of the meanings of the word atonement in the Hebrew language is "covered." The sins were not fully forgiven at that time, they were simply stored up and covered. Under the Old Covenant, believers were putting faith in a full removal of their sin that would occur in the distant future. It is for this reason that upon first seeing Jesus, John the Baptist prophesied to the crowd, "Behold the Lamb of God who takes away the sin of the world." He was telling them that all the sins they had stored up for years . . . all the days they had gone to the temple and made sacrifice to cover their sin . . . here was the Lamb who was going to take that sin away. John was telling them that this was the one in which they had believed.

The Reconciler had come. This Lamb of God was going to take away all sin. The breach would be filled by the blood of the Lamb. In writing to his young protégé, Paul wrote, "For there is only one God and one mediator who can reconcile God and people. He is the man Jesus Christ. He gave His life to purchase freedom for everyone" (1 Tim 2:5 NLT). He bore our sins in His body on the cross. He healed the breach by taking away the offense. By taking on the offense of sin, he paid the price of that sin and brought us back to the Father. God didn't just look the other way and forgive our sin. On the cross, the Lamb of God became sin for us and suffered the offense, the separation, of that sin. He was separated from the Father so that we might be brought back to the Father.

RECONCILED

The basic meaning of the word reconcile is to make friendly again or to win over to a friendly attitude. We have been made friendly with God. He has a friendly attitude towards us. If the average Christian could ever get that into their thinking, it would bring great liberation. But God's reconciliation goes even further. God not only has a friendly attitude towards us, He has a Fatherly attitude towards us. He adopted us into His family.

Reconciliation also means to settle a quarrel. Sin created an offense between God and us, which put us at odds with Him. *The Cambridge English Dictionary* defines reconcile as "to find a way in which two situations or beliefs that are opposed to each other can agree and exist together." Jesus is that Way. In John

14:6, Jesus says, "I am the Way, the Truth, and the Life. No one comes to the Father except through Me." He came and reconciled us to God by becoming our sin sacrifice.

Adam and Eve violated our fellowship with God in the Garden of Eden. But our relationship with God is also violated by our own choices. We can blame Adam and Eve for its initiation, but our own choices have sustained that violation. Before coming to Christ, we had a sinful nature. But we also had a sinful lifestyle. For that reason, we cannot come to Jesus on our own merits. We are sinful sinners. We come just as we are—with all our sins and offenses—and in His great love; He loves us. Our very sinful nature is proof of the existence of the violation of the fellowship. Listen to Romans 5:19 again, "For as by one man's disobedience many were made sinners, so also by one Man's obedience, many will be made righteous." We were made righteous and brought back into relationship with God by Christ's sacrificial death. 2 Corinthians 5:21 is one of the most liberating verses in the Bible. "He made Him who knew no sin to be sin for us, that we might become the righteousness of God in Him."

Our human nature is sinful, but when we come to Christ, we get a new nature. Paul beautifully illustrated this point a few verses earlier when he stated, "Therefore, if anyone is in Christ, he is a new creation; old things have passed away; behold, all things have become new. Now all things are of God, who has reconciled us to Himself through Jesus Christ." When you came to Christ, your old, sin nature died.

Because of that sinful nature, we were born natural enemies of God. We had fallen from the glorious relationship that God had intended. Romans 3:23 tells us that all have sinned and fallen short of God's glory. Eugene Peterson's paraphrase, *The Message*, words it beautifully: "Since we've compiled this long and sorry record as sinners (both us and them) and proved that we are utterly incapable of living the glorious lives that God wills for us." We have compiled a long and sorry sin record.

We not only inherited a sinful nature from our ancestors, Adam and Eve, we personally tasted sin ourselves. By following our "natural tendencies," we managed to compile this extensive and regrettable record. According to the Book of Revelation, this record is stored in heaven, and on Judgment Day, those record books will be opened. All the deeds recorded there will be exposed. If our name is not written in the Lamb's Book of Life, we will be judged by what is recorded in that long and sorry record.

THE PEACE OF RECONCILIATION

When man fell, he took all of creation with him. He had been given dominion over all the earth. When he bowed his knee to Satan and his lies, he submitted his dominion to Satan. In Matthew 13, Jesus makes it clear that Satan is the enemy of God. When Adam submitted to Satan, he became part of the kingdom of darkness that is at enmity with God. The Lamb of God reconciled the breach and provided peace with God for us.

Paul expresses this peace-making beautifully in his letter to the church at Colossae. "He is the image of the invisible God, the firstborn of all creation. For by Him, all things were created, in heaven and on earth, visible and invisible, whether thrones or dominions or rulers or authorities—all things were created through Him and for him. And He is before all things, and in Him all things hold together. And He is the head of the body, the church. He is the beginning, the firstborn from the dead, that in everything He might be preeminent. For in Him all the fullness of God was pleased to dwell, and through Him to reconcile to himself all things, whether on earth or in heaven, making peace by the blood of his cross" (Col 1:15-20 ESV). Through Christ, God reconciled everything to Himself. He made peace with everything in heaven and on earth by means of His blood on the cross. We, who were once so far away from God, were included in His peacemaking. We were His enemies, separated from Him by our evil thoughts and actions, yet now Christ has brought us back as His friends.

He has done this through the death of His human body on the cross. As a result, He has provided the way for us into the very

93

presence of God. We are holy and blameless as we stand before Him without a single fault. If we can ever get the truth of that last phrase into our hearts—not just our minds—it will change how we live. When we come to realize that we are holy and blameless before the throne of God—that He sees no fault in us—we will see freedom and boldness arise from within. We stand before God without fault, without a weakness, without a sin, without an offense. We no longer need to fear God! He has removed our sin completely and reconciled us back to Himself.

When Adam sinned, creation was drawn into the curse. It was not creation's fault. People often question how a God of love would allow tornadoes and other natural disasters to occur. The reason is a matter of allegiance. Adam had full authority over creation. When he bowed his knee to the Destroyer, he submitted his authority to the enemy and allowed corruption to enter creation. Even though creation was an unwilling participant, it was brought under the dominion of destruction and decay. Although creation did not play a part in the Fall, it suffers the consequences of that act.

Likewise, when Jesus reconciled everything back to himself, creation was included in that reconciliation. If the church fully understood reconciliation, we would begin reconciling creation. Ecology would be birthed in the church – not in a natural way, but in a supernatural way. Romans 8:19 says that "the earnest expectation of the creation eagerly awaits the revealing of the sons of God." The word "revealing" in this passage speaks of manifesting, expressing, or possessing our position of authority. If we substitute the word possessing for revealing, we find a whole new meaning to that passage: creation eagerly awaits the sons of God possessing and walking in their blood-bought authority. Creation is waiting for the church to activate and express its position of authority. Creation is not waiting for God to move; it is waiting for believers to move!

The verse says that "creation itself is waiting for the revealing of the sons of God." Creation is not waiting for God to reveal us. It is waiting for us to come to the understanding that we are

94

children of God. As sons of God, we are rulers upon this earth. We should be blessing creation! Obviously, that manifestation will not be completed in perfection until Christ returns. But for now, "we all, with unveiled face beholding the glory of the Lord, are being transformed into the same image from one degree of glory to another" (2 Cor 3:18 ESV).

Remember what Colossians 1:19 says: "For God and all His fullness was pleased to live in Christ. And through Him, God reconciled everything to Himself. He made peace with everything in heaven and on earth by means of His blood on the cross" (NLT). You, who were once so far away from God, were included in His peacemaking. You were His enemies, separated from Him by your evil thoughts and actions. Yet now, He has brought you back as His friends. He has done this through the death of His human body on the cross. As a result, He has brought you into the very presence of God. "You are holy and blameless as you stand before Him without a single fault" (Col 1:22 NLT).

He made peace with everything in heaven and on earth. If you can get the truth of that last phrase into your heart – not just your mind—your spiritual boldness will grow. When you come to realize that you are holy and blameless before the throne of God—that He sees no fault in you—you will see freedom and boldness arise from within. You stand before God without fault, without a weakness, without a sin, without an offense. We no longer need to fear God! He has removed our sin completely and reconciled us back to Himself.

THE PROCESS OF RECONCILIATION

The process of reconciliation is the process of restoration. The Bible is the greatest love story ever written in that it is the story of lost love restored. Humans were created as recipients of God's love. Love was lost in that traitorous act in the Garden of Eden. Jesus said that He came to "seek and to save that which was lost" (Luke 19:10). When we read the word "save", we tend to immediately think of forgiveness of sins and entrance into heaven. But the word really means to deliver, to restore, or to make whole. Jesus came to restore and make whole the relationship between God and man.

It is important to note that He did not say that He came to seek and save "those" who are lost. He said that he came to restore "that" which was lost. In the Garden, the love relationship between God and man was destroyed. As was previously stated, man's sin created a breach in the relationship. Since the quarrel was between God and man, only God and man could restore the relationship. It is for that reason that the Son of God came to earth as the Son of Man. He came to reunite the two parties.

The process of reconciliation begins when one party desires restoration of the relationship. Since God created mankind for relationship, He deeply desired the restoration of that relationship. But desire alone is not enough. The desirous party must have the ability to actively cause the restoration. Even though man may seemingly express a desire for reconciliation, he has no means or ability to fulfill that desire. His sin caused the death of the relationship. He has no ability to resolve that debt of death. Only God has the ability to resolve the conflict.

To reconcile the two parties, the desire and ability must be acted upon. One party must reach out to the other party. Man had no ability to reach out to God. He was dead in his sin from birth. King David laments in Psalm 51:5, "I was brought forth in iniquity, and in sin my mother conceived me." Since the penalty for sin is death, Paul informs us that we are all "dead in our trespasses and sins" (Eph 2:1). Dead men have no ability to reconcile the relationship. Even when man has attempted to reach out to God, he has been led astray; blinded and deceived by the ruler of this age. Paul lays this out very clearly in 2 Corinthians 4:3-4. "And even if our gospel is veiled, it is veiled to those who are perishing. In their case the god of this world has blinded the minds of the unbelievers, to keep them from seeing the light of the gospel of the glory of Christ, who is the image of God" (ESV).

Even though man was dead to God, he could not overcome this inner longing for that relationship. Blaise Paschal said, "There is a God-shaped vacuum in the heart of each man which cannot be satisfied by any created thing but only by God the Creator, made known through Jesus Christ." The God-longing of the heart caused humans to make all sorts of vain attempts at filling the emptiness. They created gods of their own making. Humans "became futile in their thoughts, and their foolish hearts were darkened. Professing to be wise, they became fools, and changed the glory of the incorruptible God into an image made like corruptible man — and birds and four-footed animals and creeping things" (Rom 1:21-23).

Humans were lost in the utter hopelessness of humanity. Even if some humans possessed the desire to reconcile the relationship, they had no ability to do so. On the other hand, God has both the desire and the ability to reconcile the problem. But His desire and ability were offset by His justice. Because He is a just God, He could not simply overlook sin. The sin debt would have to be paid and only a human could pay the debt. It is for this reason that God became flesh and dwelt among us.

That is why Jesus "did not consider it robbery to be equal with God, but made Himself of no reputation, taking the form of a bondservant, and coming in the likeness of men. And being found in appearance as a man, He humbled Himself and became obedient to the point of death, even the death of the cross" (Phil 2:6-8). God so desired the restoration of relationship that He came to earth in human form. He was born of a virgin, so as not to receive the sinful nature carried in the seed of males. He lived a sinless life, resisting all temptation. Because He had no sin, He had no sin debt to pay. In that way, He could assume the responsibility for the sin debt of all mankind and pay the debt.

Paul expressed this truth poignantly in his second letter to the church at Corinth. "For our sake He made Him to be sin who knew no sin, so that in Him we might become the righteousness of God" (2 Cor 5:21 ESV). Christ fulfilled the demands of justice by His sacrificial death. Standing between the perfect righteousness of God and the utter sinfulness of man, He bridged the gap by satisfying the offense. He became sin for man so that the now-righteous man could be reconciled to the righteous God. Even while we were still sinners, separated from God, He reached out in love. "God demonstrates His own love toward us, in that while we were still sinners, Christ died for us" (Rom 5:8). He did not wait for us. He reached out His arms of love to secure our reconciliation.

The cross is the perfect picture of God reaching out in love to bridge the gap. With righteous God on one side and sinful man on the other, the cross stands in between the two, providing the way back to God in reconciliation. Jesus Himself proclaimed that He is The Way back to God and that no man can be reconciled to God except through Him (John 14:6). Man and God could not be reconciled until the offense was removed. That offense has been removed through Christ's death on the cross. Our relationship with God is now as though there had never been an offense. He never brings it up again.

This reconciliation brings with it a certain peace in our being. We who were once enemies are now at peace — not just peace in the sense of the absence of war, but peace in the sense of entering a state of rest. The word translated as "peace" speaks of a position of rest that is receiving all the blessings of God in full assurance. It is for this reason that Jesus is called the Prince of Peace. He became a curse for us so that we might receive the blessings of Abraham.

By following our sinful nature, we have fallen short of God's intended glory. As stated earlier, God created humans as His imagers. He breathed His life into us, and that life is the life of God. Jesus came to restore that glory. In the Garden shortly before His crucifixion, Jesus prayed for us. That prayer is recorded in John 17. In verse 22, we find these life-altering words, "The glory which you gave me, I have given them, that they may be one just as we are One." He has not just removed our sin: He has positioned us to receive the intended glory. So, we are led to ask, "What is that glory that the Father gave to

Him?" John 1:14 defines that glory. "And the Word became flesh and dwelt among us, and we beheld His glory, the glory as of the only begotten of the Father, full of grace and truth." He has given us that same glory. As believers, we receive the glory of being sons of God. As sons created as His imagers, we are called to the ministry of reconciliation.

Jesus came to earth to reconcile man with God. In Paul's second letter to the church at Corinth, he said that we are given the *ministry of reconciliation*. We were reconciled to God, and now we are given the responsibility of reconciling others to Him. In this passage, Paul gives us a clear portrayal of the ministry of reconciliation. We are commissioned with the task of bringing men, women, and children back to God. "God has given us this task of reconciling people to Him. For God was in Christ, reconciling the world to himself, no longer counting people's sins against them. And he gave us this wonderful message of reconciliation. So, we are Christ's ambassadors; God is making his appeal through us. We speak for Christ when we plead, 'Come back to God!'" (2 Cor 5:18-20 NLT).

THE MINISTRY OF RECONCILIATION

In 1975, my friend Jimmy Draper was a pastor of First Baptist Church in Dallas, Texas. In his book, *Say Neighbor—Your House is on Fire!*[5], Jimmy relates the story of coming home late one night and finding his neighbor's house on fire. When he arrived, he expected to see fire and rescue vehicles, but they had not yet arrived. He was the first on the scene. The fire had started in the garage, and the family was asleep at the other end of the house. Jimmy ran to the front door of the house and began pounding on the door.

Eventually, he saw the features of the two youngest children appear in the translucent glass of the door's sidelight. He identified himself and encouraged them to open the door. They tried, but their little fingers could not manage the latches.

[5] James T. Draper, Say Neighbor – Your House is on Fire!, (Dallas: Crescendo Book Publications, 1975)

Finally, the older daughter appeared and unlocked the door. She then ran to her parents' bedroom and awakened them. The whole family managed to escape as the house filled with suffocating smoke.

In the book, Jimmy uses this event to stimulate believers to share the gospel with their neighbors. Our neighbor's lives are on fire. They are in peril of perishing without hope unless someone rescues them. It did not matter to Jimmy that the family was tired from a busy day. It did not matter that they were sleeping comfortably in their cozy beds. Their house was on fire, and they must be warned. It did not matter that Jimmy was tired after a long day of ministry. The neighbor's house was on fire. Regardless of the inconvenience, He was compelled to warn them.

Because the God of love has placed His life essence in us, we are compelled by love. If love compels us, how can we possibly keep from telling others that their spiritual house is on fire? Evangelism is not about data; it is about love. Our evangelism, or lack thereof, is a direct barometer of our love. If we really love God, and we really love others, we will share what we have. The Bible tells us to love our neighbor as ourselves. If we loved that deeply, is there any possible way that we could let our neighbor go to hell without showing him The Way? If I really loved the person next door, I would make sure that I did everything within my power to see them reconciled to God. There's a chance that they will reject my message, and they could possibly even get mad at me. They may tell me they are too busy or that they have plenty of time later. They may tell me not to say anything else to them about Jesus. But on judgment day, my hands will be clean.

We try to warn them, and that is all we can do. In the story of Jimmy's neighbor, he relates that he first tried to kick the door in. But it was a solid core door with three locks. What a clear reminder that God has not called us to kick the door down. Kicking down doors is not something he does. He stands at the door and knocks. He has called us to simply warn our friends and family of the impending danger. The fires of hell are getting

100

closer and closer. They must be warned. If they will not heed the warning, on judgment day, our love will be hurt as we watch them banished.

At that moment, we will have been transformed. Our mortality will have put on immortality. Our old, corrupted physical body will have been replaced with an incorruptible body. We will experience the washing away of our sins and bask in the perfect love of God. But in that moment, there will be an offense to our love as we see people we know ushered out of the judgment hall and into eternal damnation. We are already forgiven, so there will be no condemnation. But there will be an offense to the love that is in us when we watch them herded away.

I often visualize how that will feel. I imagine some distant friend looking at me with intense fear in his eyes. As he realizes that I knew the answer, he asks, "You knew. You knew this was coming, and you didn't warn me! Why didn't you care enough to warn me? I thought we were friends." How much easier to bear, if that person says, "You knew. You were right. You tried to warn me. I would not listen. It is my fault. I should have listened to you."

That scene is quite possibly what Scripture means when it says, "He will wipe away every tear" (Rev 21:4). He did not say we would not cry, but rather that He would dry our eyes. Have you ever wondered why we are crying? Perhaps we are crying over the wounding of our love; watching people we know banished from the presence of God and herded into eternal darkness.

As ambassadors of reconciliation, our task is to show people the way back to God. Imagine a large chasm between two cliffs. We will call one cliff, the Human Cliff. The other we will call the God Cliff. Remember, between these two cliffs is an infinitely deep, insurmountable chasm. Imagine Jesus standing in the midst of this vast breach. He has stretched forth one arm to grasp the Man Cliff, and his other arm is holding onto the God Cliff. His body. Thus stretched out, He forms a cross. This cross is the bridge over the insurmountable chasm. Our task is to simply grasp people by the hand and lead them across the bridge. We do not have to provide the bridge; Jesus is the bridge. We do not have to pray for God to provide a way—He has already done so. He simply needs someone to go and bring the people to the bridge. Jesus said, "I am the Way, the Truth, the Life; no man comes to the Father but by Me" (John 14:6). Our assignment is to encourage people to go through the Way and back to God. Ours is the ministry of reconciliation.

Brother Leonard Ravenhill used to tell us, "This generation of believers is responsible for this generation of lost." We will have to give an account for every lost man who does not hear the gospel of Jesus Christ. If we do not implore our neighbors to be reconciled to God, who will? It is our assignment. Nowhere in the New Testament does it say to pray for your lost friends to get saved. In Acts 4, we find the Church in the upper room praying for the expansion of the gospel. They never prayed, "Lord God, save people." They prayed, "Lord God, let Your miraculous power flow through us so that we will have the boldness to preach the good news of reconciliation!" Within a few months of Calvary, the church in Jerusalem had grown to thousands of members. Those early believers understood they had a responsibility to take their neighbors, friends, and family across the bridge. That task has not changed.

We have been reconciled to God. Our offense was removed by Christ when He became sin for us and gave us His righteousness. Our account in heaven was justified. We are not just forgiven; our sins have been removed from our account and placed into Jesus' account. It is as though we have never sinned. It is as though we had never tasted evil and as if Adam and Eve had never eaten that fruit. There is no barrier between God and us. But we must not forget that we have been commissioned to share this reconciliation with the world.

William Booth, the founder of the Salvation Army, once had a vision of the drowning lost. He saw a dark, stormy sea with dark clouds hanging over it. Occasionally, lightning flashed, accompanied by deafening thunder. In this dark, tumultuous sea, he saw thousands of people thrashing around, struggling to keep from drowning. They would eventually sink below the surface of the dark sea, never to rise again.

Rising out of the dark sea was a mighty rock whose summit reached way above the dark clouds. All around the base of the rock was a boardwalk. A number of the poor, hopeless people managed to reach the boardwalk and climb out of the deadly sea. As he looked more closely at the scene, he realized that some of those who had escaped the sea were working diligently to rescue the poor drowning people. They were throwing ropes to people and attaching ladders to the boardwalk. Some were even jumping back into the sea at their own peril to rescue others. But the number of those working to rescue the perishing was only a small portion of the inhabitants of the boardwalk.

Even though they had all been rescued from the deadly sea at some point, they appeared to have forgotten all the pain and suffering they experienced in the sea. They seemed to be unconcerned about the drowning masses. This unconcern surely could not have been based on ignorance. The struggling, drowning people were well within eyesight, many just a few feet from the boardwalk. Many of those on the boardwalk even gathered to sing songs and hear lectures about the plight of the poor, drowning people. Often, they would enter a time of prayer, asking God to help them be happier.

Then they would return to the activities that absorbed their time. Some worked in their garden, some painted pictures, othes read books, or listened to music. Many were involved day and night in gaining resources they would store in boxes. They themselves had been rescued at some point, but did nothing to help rescue the countless masses drowning in the dark sea.

As believers, we have been rescued and our relationship reconciled so that we might rescue those around us that are drowning in sin and rebellion. We are reconciled, and now we have the ministry of reconciliation. The founder of the Navigators, Dawson Trotman, wrote a little booklet called *Born to Reproduce*. In that booklet, Dawson explains that Adam was created to reproduce. The Lord commanded him to be fruitful and multiply. He was to fill the earth. The same command was given to Noah when he exited the ark. We are born again as God's new creation, and the same command is given to us: be fruitful and multiply. Jesus commanded us to go make disciples of all nations. In other words, we are to be fruitful and multiply We are to fill the earth with children of God.

We have been reconciled to God by His great love. We are ambassadors of that love. God has given us love because He has given us Himself, and He is love. Because He is in you, love is in you, and that love compels you to rescue others. Christ's love in us compels us to use every means we can to rescue as many people as we can. In 2 Corinthians 5:14, Paul tells us that Christ's love controls him. That is the foundation of the ministry of reconciliation; letting Christ's love control you.

During a trip to Asia years ago, we discovered that a city-wide transportation strike had been called. We were on our return leg home, and our Kathmandu hotel was about a two-hour walk from the airport. So, we planned to hire some locals to help carry our bags through the city to the airport the next morning. That evening, our team gathered together and prayed for the two parties to reach reconciliation. We prayed that the government and the transportation people would come to an agreement that would end the strike. I was so confident that God would reconcile the situation that I asked our taxi driver if he would pick us up the next morning.

"Oh, no," he replied. "Transportation strike in the morning."

Without hesitation, I said, "That strike has been called off."

"How do you know?" he asked inquisitively.

"We prayed," I replied.

With a smirk on his face, he said, "Sure, we prayed too. We all prayed. But there will still be a strike in the morning."

"But our God is all-powerful and will reconcile the parties," I stated confidently. That pretty well ended the conversation.

We were awakened the next morning to the sound of taxi horns on the streets. The number of vehicles on the streets was steadily growing. Because much of their communication was by word of mouth in those days, one taxi driver spoke to another driver to inform him that the two sides had been reconciled. In turn, he also spread the word to other drivers. What a wonderful picture of authentic evangelism. The love of God in you compelling you to inform others that the two sides have reconciled: God and man are now at peace.

The church in the New Testament had no training courses in evangelism and no gospel tracts. They New Testament had not even been written. All they possessed was a love for God and a love for others. They saw their friends and family sinking into the dark sea and risked everything to rescue them. Jesus had commanded that they love others as He loved them. He laid down His life for them, so they laid down their life. The love of God controlled them, and they turned the world upside down.

All this is God's doing,
for he has reconciled us to himself through Jesus Christ;
and he has made us agents of the reconciliation.
God was in Christ personally reconciling the world to
himself—not counting their sins against them—and has
commissioned us with the message of reconciliation.
We are now Christ's ambassadors,
as though God were appealing direct to you through us.
As his personal representatives we say,
"Make your peace with God."
For God caused Christ,
who himself knew nothing of sin,
actually to be sin for our sakes,
so that in Christ we might be made good
with the goodness of God.
2 Corinthians 5:18-21 (Phillips)[6]

---

[6] J. B. Phillips, ed., *The New Testament in Modern English* (New York: HarperCollins, 1960).

6

AMBASSADORS
OF LOVE

"I have found the paradox, that if you love until it hurts,
there can be no more hurt, only more love."
— *Mother Teresa*

As the driver started the engine and the Land Rover inched its way down the path, they reached through the window for one last touch—one more handclasp, one more eye to eye. With tears flowing down their faces, they blew the kisses of goodbye. What human language was incapable of expressing, they said with their eyes, "I love you. I love you."

As the Land Rover picked up speed they had to release their hands from the door and content themselves with waving. That last view will be forever imprinted upon my heart. As we disappeared around a turn, I could see them standing in front of the little, block church and grass huts . . . still waving, still giving their love.

I had gone to that little village in southeastern Nepal to teach the great truths of God's Word. But in the course of time, I had been taught the greatest of all truths. "They'll know we are His disciples by our love."

We Americans have made Christianity into an intellectual endeavor. Teaching as if we were the ultimate authorities on the subject, we have our own pet doctrines and sub-doctrines. We have so much knowledge and so little understanding. We have learned the words of the Bible, but have seemingly failed to hear its voice. Frequently, we as humans possess the data but fail to grasp the true principle.

The year is 1875, and the old scribe made his way into the familiar quarters of the Parisian artist, Marcel de Leclure. Finding his well-worn perch behind the ornate desk, he readied himself for another day of ink and paper. For more days than he cared to remember, he had been under contract to the artist. Hour upon hour, day after day, he had faithfully recorded the words of his employer. All this investment of time had been expended on one simple project—a love letter to Marcel de Leclure's aristocratic flame, Magdalene de Villalore.

"Shall we continue with the letter or begin something new," the old man queried.

"Nay, Nay, sir. Until my love is faithfully and fully communicated to this one who holds my heart, there is nothing else. She must know the depths of my love," the artist replied. "Read to me my last words."

"Je vous aime," the scribe heartlessly responded.

"Je vous aime. Ah yes, je vous aime." He savored the words with his tongue as though he were enjoying the bouquet of a vintage wine. "Je vous aime. . . je vous aime. . . write scribe, write. Not one word is to be missed."

Again and again, the old scribe recorded the words "Je vous aime." Until, in the end, the phrase was written exactly 1,875,000 times—a thousand times the calendar year of the writing. Every word written was lovingly and passionately spoken by the artist and then recorded in the voluminous letter. But hearing himself speak the words was not enough. Marcel de Leclure had the scribe read the entire letter back to him—word for word. Before the letter was even sent, the words "jevous aime" ("I love you") were spoken some five and a half million times. What a magnificent display of love! What expenditure of expression! What a clear voice of his heart!

The Bible comprises sixty-six books, covers several thousand years, and contains some 775,000 words. The scope of its audience is much larger than Marcel de Leclure's, but its message is the same. From Genesis through Revelation, God is saying over and over, "I love you! I love you! I love you!!!" From generation to generation, the message is the same, "I love you! I love you! I love you!!!"

Before the "beginning," there was love. If we could somehow gaze through a "time-telescope" into the past, we would see love. Before anything existed, there was love. The Bible opens with the words, "In the beginning, God." The Apostle John is referred to as the Apostle of Love. His first letter to the Church is often referred to as the Epistle of Love. In 1 John 4:16, he writes that "God is love." So if God was in the beginning, love was in the beginning. John goes so far as to write, "He who abides in love, abides in God, and God in him." Therefore, without violating the Genesis text we could read those first few words as, "In the beginning, love . . ."

As a matter of fact, love was not only present in the beginning, love was the very reason for the beginning. God who is love personified, was alone in eternity past. There was nothing in existence like Him with whom He could have relationship, so He created man. He created man in His own image to enable the expression of His love through a living relationship. He created a creation that could love back.

A small child was clutching a baby doll to her chest. With tears in her eyes, she looked up at her mother and cried, "I love them and love them, but they never love me back." Creator God had no desire to create puppets or dolls—He wanted lovers. So, he created humans.

Man was created as the authority of this world, so it was essential this new creation be created from materials of this realm. When God created man, He created him out of the dust of the ground. After forming this container for His greatest creation, God breathed into him the "breath of life." But what was that "breath of life?" The "breath of life" is that quality that makes man "like God." Most agree that this "breath" is the very essence of God. God breathed His very essence into man, and man became a living being. And what was this essence of God? Love is the essence of God that gives life to man.

THE VERY ESSENCE OF GOD

In his first letter to the church, John, the apostle of love, reveals this truth: that love is the very essence of God. Love is more than an attribute or characteristic of God. God is love. Love flavors everything He does because love is His essential being. If there is no Love, there is no God of the Bible. 1 John 4:8 tells us that "God is love." Notice that John did not say that God has love or even that God loves. He said, "God is love." Love is at the very core of His being. When God breathed His essence into man, He breathed Love into man.

Jesus is the Son of God and, as such, is the Son of Love. We can get a broader understanding of this truth by looking at John 1:1. "In the beginning the Word already existed, He was with God, and He was God. He was in the beginning with God. He created everything there is. Nothing exists that He didn't make" (NLT). Since God is love, let us again make a word substitution. "In the beginning, the Word already existed, He was with Love, and He was Love. He was in the beginning with Love. Love created everything there is. Nothing exists that Love didn't create." This Love took on human form and dwelt here upon this earth as Jesus of Nazareth. Jesus' life was a life of love. Everything He did was motivated by love. How often do we read that He was moved with compassion? Love was His very essence. This love was the very source of life for Him.

Love is the source of life for us all. When God breathed into man the breath of life, He was truly breathing Love into man. When man chose to sin, he lost this love relationship. He died in his love relationship with God. Jesus, the Son of Love, came to restore this life of love. Again, John, the beloved apostle, helps us in this matter. In John 1:4 he writes, "In Him (Love) was life, and the life was the light of every man." Verse 9 goes on to say that this light of Love enlightens every person. Every person has some measure of love within them. God, who is Love, has given it to them. It is for this reason that the book of Romans tells us that all mankind is without excuse. We are without excuse because we have all been touched by Love.

A life without love is not really life – it is deprivation. It is mere existence. None of us even want to imagine what it would be like to live life in the total absence of love. Everything we know is stamped with the mark of the Loving Creator. Life that is void of that love is not life – it is hell! Life that is full of love is heaven on earth. "God is love, and all who live in love live in God, and God lives in them. And as we live in God, our love grows more perfect" (1 John 4:16 NLT).

This Love always was . . . it has no beginning . . . it already existed in the beginning. As surely as that is true, so it is that Love never ends. Love never dies. 1 Corinthians 13:8 tells us that love will last forever. Love is eternal because God is eternal. He is the alpha and the omega, the beginning and the end. When everything began, Love already existed, and when everything in this physical realm is finished, Love will continue on. An article in the now defunct magazine, *Ladies Home Journal,* once stated, "Those who love deeply never grow old; they may die of old age, but they die young."

Not only is love eternal, but it is also tangible. It can be seen and heard and felt. Jesus was the personification of this Love. Everything He did, He did for Love. He didn't heal the sick so people would know that He was powerful. Most often, He told the person healed not to even tell anyone.

His purpose wasn't to convince people to follow Him by healing the sick. He healed the sick because He was Love personified. Due to His great love, He healed Jairus' daughter. He even told her parents not to tell anyone what had happened.

One can only imagine the pressure this placed on those parents. They just experienced love personified. Jesus was "touchable" love, and that Love had touched them. And yet they were asked not to tell anyone about the experience.

Once more, John has something to say about this. The key word in his first letter to the church is "love." We know Love is the one thing that existed from the beginning, for God is Love. Therefore, let's do a little word substitution again. "The Love who existed from the beginning is the Love we have heard and seen. We saw Love with our own eyes and touched Him with our own hands. He is Jesus Christ, the Word of life. This one who is life from Love was shown to us, and we have seen Love" (1 John 1:1 NLT substitution adds).

Love demands tangible expression. As surely as the wind cannot blow without giving tangible evidence of its presence, love cannot exist without tangible expression. God created man in His very own image, and in so doing, He created man alone. At the close of each creation day, God surveyed His work and proclaimed, "It is good!" On the sixth day, He created man, and at the close of that day, He surveyed His handiwork — man in His own image. For the first time in the creation event, He proclaimed, "It is not good! It is not good that man should live alone." God had created into man the same "loneness" that He possessed personally. So, God created woman to complete man's love. He did not give him another man to try to complete him. He created woman as the perfect completion of the love creation.

LOVE DEMANDS EXPRESSION

We know from personal experience that love demands expression. It is impossible to hide love. Trying to hide love is like trying to hide a halogen light in a straw hat. As surely as the light peeps out through the cracks, love will not go unexpressed. When a young girl first experiences love, she has to express it. She is not content to just "love" that little, freckle-faced lad. She has to express it. She has to let it "slip" to her girlfriends that she

112

likes little Johnny. Of course, she tells them not to tell anyone but would "die" if they didn't.

And poor little Johnny wants to let her know that the feeling is mutual. But the boys will not be as understanding and cooperative as her girlfriends. He tries to pretend "no interest." But his heart is bursting to let her know. So, in elementary, clandestine operations, he sends her a text or slips her a note, hoping the guys never find out. He willingly runs the risk of utter humiliation and peer torment because his love demands expression.

Love is not only expressive, it is also active. Love without action is not really love at all, but is nothing more than empty words and childish emotions. With an act of our will, we release the Love that is within us. This release is always active. Psychologists tell us that when two people are in love, one is the "lover" and one is the "lovee." But love is not passively allowing another to love you — it is actively loving another. Everything we know about love has to do with God's love in us. "We know what real love is because Christ gave up his life for us. And so, we also ought to give up our lives for our Christian brothers and sisters. But if anyone has enough money to live well and sees a brother or sister in need and refuses to help – how can God's love be in that person? Dear children, let us stop just saying we love each other; let us really show it by our actions" (1 John 3:16-18 NLT).

Fear keeps us from acting on our love. We are afraid of rejection or ridicule. We are sometimes even afraid of love itself—afraid of what love will do to us; how it will change us. But real love breaks through the fear—it throws off the fear. True love is trustworthy. It is worthy of our trust. When we live in love, we live in security. According to 1 Corinthians 13, love does not force itself on others and is not judgmental. Love is a secure resting place for our peace. When love settles in, fear and judgment retreat.

God desires for us to live in this place of security—knowing that He loves us and that His love abides in us. For too long, the church has dwelt in a house of fear. Fear and love cannot coexist.

Look at the words of 1 John 4:16. "We know how much God loves us, and we have put our trust in Him. God is love, and all who live in love live in God, and God lives in them. And as we live in God, our love grows more perfect. So, we will not be afraid on the day of judgment, but we can face Him with confidence because we are like Christ here in this world. Such love has no fear because perfect love expels all fear. If we are afraid, it is for fear of judgment, and this shows that His love has not been perfected in us" (NLT).

This perfect love of God is not pretentious or showy by nature. God is not always talking about His love—He simply demonstrates His love. Real love is never showy. It is simple and secure. I don't have many memories of my dad hugging me and telling me he loved me as I was growing up. That just wasn't his style. One of the few times I do remember, I was already grown. At my ordination into the ministry, Dad laid his hands on my head and whispered in my ear, "I love you, and I am proud of you." That was probably the longest discourse I ever heard from him on love and acceptance. But he said it in so many other ways. An example is the time my car broke down on my way home from work. I was in college and working on the railroad, and I worked the late night shift. My car broke down on the way home in the early morning hours. I called him, and he came and towed me home—even though he had to get up in a couple of hours and go to work himself. Even though I was married and on my own, he still came to my assistance. Throughout my years of playing sports, I was never more than average. But he never showed any disappointment. He just accepted the facts as they were. I never remember getting into his truck after a game and hearing him lecture me on how I should have done better. He didn't have to talk about love and acceptance—he simply lived it out.

So, it is with our Heavenly Father. He loves us with an unpretentious, genuine love. A love that is honest and open—loving just as we are. And that is the way He expects us to love others. Genuine love is a precious commodity in our world of "virtual" love that looks so real but ends when your dollar runs out. The impersonal societies in which we live contribute to a cheap form of love that talks a good game but never delivers. But the Love we have received from God is genuine and pure. As His representatives here on earth, He expects the love we express to be just as genuine and pure.

A CONSUMING FIRE

Genuine love is a consuming thing. It starts so small . . . just a little glint of light in the darkness of the soul. In romantic love, it may be that casual glance from across the room that catches the eye or that deeper "eye-to-eye" contact that communicates interest. Whatever the source, a small fire has been ignited. A fire that will continue to grow until it is extinguished or has consumed all that is.

On the other hand, it may be that little feeling of hope way down deep that says, "All is not lost. All is not hopeless. Something larger than you or your problems is here." From that vague feeling of comfort, a fire is lit. . . a fire that calls out for a deeper experience of Love. True love is never satisfied; it always craves more love. It is a dynamic – ever-growing or slowly dying. That is why the Scriptures say that our God is a "consuming fire." The deeper our relationship with Him, the deeper we want it to grow. Paul, the apostle, was in such communion with God that he had been caught up into the third heaven. Yet, he writes that he is pressing in, toward a deeper love relationship with God. Even though he walked in such deep revelation and relationship that a spirit was allowed to buffet him to keep him humble, he expressed his desire to really "know Christ and experience the mighty power that raised Him from the dead" (Phil 3:10 NLT).

That is what happens in romantic relationships. We feel that spark of love in our heart for the other person and we desire to spend time with them—enjoying their presence. But the more time we spend with them, the more time we want to spend. Then, we come to that place where our desire is to spend the rest of our lives together, and we marry them. But it doesn't stop there, it just really begins there. After fifty-plus years of marriage, I fall more deeply in love with Delores every day. True love is a consuming thing. God is never satisfied with partial love. "And do you suppose God doesn't care? The proverb has it that "he's a fiercely jealous love" (James 4:5 MESS).

THE COMFORT OF LOVE

But in the midst of this raging fire of love, there is a certain and definite comfortableness. Years ago, I heard a teaching on the three levels of love: because, if, and period. "Because" love says, "I love you because you drive a cool car," or "I love you because you make a lot of money," or "I love you because you are successful." This kind of love is the most elementary since it loves because of the things the relationship will bring – fame, fortune, etc. "If" love is a controlling love. It says, "I'll love you if you do such-and-such." It may be worded in an even more controlling way—"If you loved me, you would do such-and-such" or "If you loved me, you wouldn't do such-and-such." Whichever the case, this kind of love is used to manipulate and control the other person. True love never behaves itself in such a crass manner. True love says, "I love you period—no "ifs" or "becauses."

This kind of love is comfortable because it accepts us just as we are—frailties and all. There are no conditions to be met. No changes are required. This unconditional love is what God has given us. He doesn't wait for us to change our lives and quit all our bad habits before He loves us. He loves us as we are. Any personal improvements we make will in no way influence the depth of His love. And any personal failures will in no way hinder His love. He loves us, period.

This kind of love brings forth a deep restoration in our soul. When we know that our acceptance is not dependent upon our performance, we perform at a higher level. Back in 1964, the St. Louis Cardinals baseball team made a last-minute player trade with the Chicago Cubs. As part of the deal, St. Louis received outfielder Lou Brock, who was barely an average player. When

Brock landed in St. Louis, the Cardinals were in fourth place with no real hopes of winning the pennant. But Brock blossomed in St. Louis. His batting average soared into the .300's, and he became such a tremedous base-stealing threat. Hall of Fame pitcher, Don Drysdale, said this about him, "You knew he was going to steal, but there was nothing you could do to stop it." Brock's performance led the Cardinals to the National League pennant that year. From there, they went on to win the World Series, becoming the 1964 world champions. What made the difference in Lou Brock's performance?

It seems that the difference was the manner in which the two clubs handled mistakes. The Cubs organization spent time after every game analyzing every mistake made. Mistakes cost ball games, and Chicago used a system to figure out why the mistakes were made and then implemented chages to eliminate the mistakes. Brock reported that with the Cardinals it was different. The organization expected mistakes. You had a right to fail. You had the freedom to make mistakes. That freedom turned Lou Brock into one of Baseball's all-time greats. The Lou Brock Award is given every year to the player with the most stolen bases in Major League Baseball. And in 1985, Lou Brock was inducted into baseball's Hall of Fame. Listen to what he said about the fear of failure—"Show me a man who's afraid to look bad, and I will show you a man I can beat every time."

God's love is comfortable with our failures. Knowing human frailty, He knows we are going to make mistakes. He knows it so well that He sent His son to die for those mistakes. He understands that the only man who doesn't fail is the man who doesn't try. Oh, did I mention that Lou Brock also averaged 100 strikeouts per season—the highest for any lead-off hitter in baseball?

Once you settle into the comfortableness of love, you find the barriers coming down. All of us have them, to one degree or another — those protective shields around our heart. These shields have been placed there over the years to protect our hearts. When the Bible talks about "guarding our hearts" this is definitely NOT what it is talking about. These shields are deposits of unforgiveness that form thick, calloused barriers over our wounded areas. We've been hurt before, and we are not going to be hurt again.

They seem so valid. Why expose your soft spots so people can hurt you? It is for your own well-being to protect yourself. But in reality, those protections wall us off from love. They are self-preservation thoughts, and their root is selfishness. In 1 Corinthians 10, Paul addresses some of these self-preserving thoughts when he says, "We are human, but we don't wage war with human plans and methods. We use God's mighty weapons, not mere worldly weapons, to knock down the Devil's strongholds. With these weapons, we break down every proud argument that keeps people from knowing God. With these weapons, we conquer their rebellious ideas, and we teach them to obey Christ" (2 Cor 10:3-5 NLT). What are the weapons? Love and forgiveness. As we sink into the protective, comfortable covering of God's unconditional love, we find those old, self-preserving ideas falling away.

With the barriers falling, we find it easier to be transparent. The comfort of love makes us willing to give of ourselves—from the very depth of our being. But it is much more than a willingness. There is a desire to give. A desire to express this love we feel. Openly and without hesitation, we give expansively. Cost is irrelevant. We are giving of ourselves. Those outside of the relationship speak of the sacrifice, but that idea has never even entered our mind. We give cheerfully for the sheer ecstasy of giving. We have received and are continuing to receive so much that the gift we give seems insignificant—no matter the cost. Love has broken down the walls, and the Spirit of Love is flowing through our lives. We are alive like we have never been alive before. There is no greater peace than resting in the unconditional love of God. This is comfort that Paul spoke of when he wrote, "The peace of God, which surpasses all understanding, will guard your hearts and minds through Christ Jesus" (Phil 4:6).

LOVE IS CONTAGIOUS

There is also a heart-pounding excitement in this love exchange. As we give and receive with the One we love, there is a deep passion growing within us. This is a dynamic passion for the One we love. But it goes far beyond just the One we love. There is a passion for life itself. Life suddenly seems worth living. We have moved from mere existence into the abundance of life that Christ promised.

We are filled with His love, and it flows from our very being. It is as though we are becoming Love at the core of our existence. Love has become our essence. This excitement and passion is much more than just simple emotion. There is a deeper movement in progress. It is a movement of commitment, wherein we pledge our very being to the one we love. This commitment is not merely an emotional response, but rather, it is an act of our will that is empowered by our love. It is a commitment not of compulsion or law; it is a commitment that is far, far deeper. It is a commitment springing forth from love and reverberating with joy. It is the cheerful giving of our all, because we want to give. And the more we give—the more we want to give. Nowhere is the teaching of reaping and sowing more apparent than in this matter of love and commitment. It is almost paradoxical. The more we commit—the more we expend—the more we have—the more we commit—the more we expend.

It is as though love is contagious. It spreads in our lives like a positive virus. This love bug infiltrates one aspect of our life, then before we know it, our entire life is infected. It's like the Energizer bunny, it just keeps going and going and going. But not only does it spread in us; it spreads from us. This love is highly contagious. This is exactly why the apostle Paul wrote that we are "ambassadors for Christ" (2 Cor 5:20). We are ambassadors of love.

This love is so totally consuming and overwhelming that it spreads from us to others. We can see this pattern or process as we chase the movement of love. Long before we loved God, He loved us. Not only did He love us first, but He did not wait for us to reciprocate His love before He began expressing His love. His love for us touched us and changed us.

It changed us at the very root of our being. This change produced love in us. He loved us and demonstrated that love for us in a powerful way. Only then did we begin to love Him. As we loved God, we found that this singular love began to spread. As Ambassadors of Love, our love was extended not only to Him but to other people as well.

As we begin to love others, they are touched with this Love that has consumed us, and they are touched. They are changed as Love touches them, and the process continues. This love is transferable. It spreads from God to man . . . from man to man . . . from land to land. . . from generation to generation . . . for eternity. For love is eternal. And we have been commissioned as ambassadors of this eternal love.

AMBASSADORS OF LOVE

In Matthew 16, Jesus is explaining to His followers what it means to follow Him. He tells his followers that if a person tries to live for himself, he will lose out on experiencing the abundance of life. But if he surrenders his life to Christ and His kingdom, he will experience this overflowing life. What a perfect definition of what it means to be an ambassador of love. Do you hear what He is saying? "If you live your life trying to please yourself—without entering into a love relationship with God—you will miss the fullness of life. But if you will live your life for Love—if you will live in the Love of God—and live loving—you will really find life in its deepest form." The abundant life that Jesus promised is simply a life filled with Love.

The true measure of our Christian life is not how much we know. It is not how well we can explain the Scriptures or how well we understand doctrine. It is not even how many good works we have performed. Faith is important, but it is useless without love. In 1 Corinthians 13:2, Paul states this very plainly. He writes, "Though I have all faith, so that I could remove mountains, but have not love, I am nothing." He concludes that chapter saying, "And now abide faith, hope, love, these three; but the greatest of these is love."

As important as faith is to our spiritual life, it is nothing without love. And who can bear living a life without hope? It is incredibly important that we have hope, but hope that isn't grounded in love will soon disappoint. The only thing that truly remains is love. The measure of our life is how much we have loved. We must always remember that we are ambassadors of love.

Paul, the apostle, first introduced this concept of being ambassadors in 2 Corinthians 5. He explained that we represent Christ and His kingdom of love to this lost and dying world. Love was the drawing force that compelled people to follow Jesus. Obviously, the miracles were also a great draw, but mystical healers were somewhat common in the Eastern world. But none broke the boundaries of religion and displayed boundless love like Jesus. What other healer willingly touched a leper? No one extended love like Jesus.

Ambassador Defined

An ambassador is most often defined as the highest-ranking diplomatic representative appointed by one government as the in-resident representative of his own government to another country or government. When Jesus commissions us to operate in His name to expand the kingdom of God, He is commissioning us as ambassadors. When Paul says that we are ambassadors for Christ, he is saying that we are the highest-ranking diplomatic representatives of the Kingdom of God.

As ambassadors, we are residents of this world but citizens of a higher kingdom. As I think about that statement, I am reminded of an old gospel song from my childhood. It was written in 1919 by an unknown author.

This world is not my home, I'm just a-passing through,
My treasures are laid up somewhere beyond the blue;
The angels beckon me from heaven's open door,
And I can't feel at home in this world anymore.

Even though we reside in the physical realm of this blue orb, this is not our home. We are citizens of heaven in residence in this foreign land as the highest-ranking diplomats of the kingdom of heaven. In a world of darkness, hatred, abuse, neglect, loneliness, and isolation, we alone are commissioned to love. That commission is founded upon that most famous of verses, John 3:16. "For God so loved the world that He gave His only begotten Son that whosoever believes in Him will not perish but have everlasting life." That is the love that we are commissioned to represent.

When we hear the word ambassador, we tend to think of great pomp and splendor—grand ballrooms, and high society. But in so doing, we are forgetting the kingdom we represent. We need to remind ourselves of the great Christian ambassadors of the past. These men and women suffered great hardship taking the message of God's love around the world. For the kingdom we represent is not of this world and does not operate by the protocols of earthly kingdoms. Christ is indeed the King of Kings and the Lord of Lords. But while living on earth, He proclaimed He did not come to be served, but to serve. His kingdom is a kingdom of love, and the greatest ambassadors in His kingdom are those who serve the most.

In the last few verses of Matthew's gospel, Jesus commissioned His followers to go make disciples of all nations in His name. They were to act as His ambassadors with the power to use His name. As His ambassadors, they were to stand in for Him and do the things that He would do if He were there. He was inviting them to live life as He lived it. Peter tells us that Jesus left us an example and that we should follow in His footsteps. Listen to how Eugene Peterson phrases Peter's admonition. "This is the kind of life you've been invited into, the

122

kind of life Christ lived. He suffered everything that came his way so you would know that it could be done, and also know how to do it, step-by-step" (1 Peter 2:20 – MESS).

A beautiful expression of what this life of love looks like can be found in the biography of the missionary Jim Elliot. Jim felt called to share this message of love with a barbaric native tribe in Ecuador. He and his fellow laborers worked hard to establish a friendly relationship by giving gifts and speaking words of kindness. Then came the day they landed their small plane on the beach of the river near the native village. Instead of receiving friendship, they encountered hostility upon their arrival.

As a spear-toting warrior approached him, Jim instinctively reached for the pistol on his belt. But then realized that was not the way his Master would respond. He and his four companions were slaughtered that day. They laid their life down willingly to exhibit the kingdom of love to this tribe. The words found written in his journal clearly define the work of Christ's ambassadors. "He is no fool who gives what he cannot keep to gain that which he cannot lose." Jesus said that whoever desires to keep his life will lose it. But the one who lays down his life in service will gain life.

AN AMBASSADOR'S LIFE AND WORK

In the last chapter, we explored our reconciliation with God. God loved the world so much that He took on human flesh and blood. He became one of us to reconcile us to Himself. In His final remarks before His arrest and crucifixion, He defined the depths of this love. He said, "There is no greater love than to lay down one's life for one's friends" (John 15:13 NLT). Christ laid down His life in heaven to live as a human. Then He laid down that human, physical life to reconcile us with God

The realization of the depths of that love causes us to stand in awe and amazement. Centuries ago, Charles Wesley expressed the sheer amazement of the depths of this love in his classic hymn, "And Can It Be, That I Should Gan?"

And can it be that I should gain
An interest in the Savior's blood?
Died He for me, who caused His pain?
For me, who Him to death pursued?
Amazing love! how can it be
That Thou, my God, should die for me?
Amazing love! how can it be
That Thou, my God, should die for me!
He left His Father's throne above,
So free, so infinite His grace;
Emptied Himself of all but love,
And bled for Adam's helpless race;
'Tis mercy all, immense and free;
For, O my God, it found out me.

We have been commissioned as ambassadors of this amazing love. As such, our main responsibility as ambassadors is to bring people back to God. Paul sets forth this task of reconciliation in 2 Corinthians 5. He writes, "And all of this is a gift from God, who brought us back to himself through Christ. And God has given us the task of reconciling people to Him. For God was in Christ, reconciling the world to himself, no longer counting people's sins against them. And he gave us this wonderful message of reconciliation" (2 Cor 18-19, NLT). This magnificent message of love has been given to us as His ambassadors to share with others. In our position as ambassadors of love, we are to stand in for Christ. As Paul continues this passage about ambassadorship, he writes, " So we are Christ's ambassadors; God is making his appeal through us. We speak for Christ when we plead, 'Come back to God!" (2 Cor 5:20 NLT).

The love of God expressed in Jesus bridged the gap between the perfect God and corrupt humanity. His cross provided the way for man to return to God. He reconciled us back to Himself, becoming the Great Mediator. Our sole responsibility, as ambassadors, is to share His love in such abundance that people are drawn to walk across that bridge into the love of God. Jesus told us that He is the Way; therefore, our task is to help people find the Way. In simplest of terms, it is our job as Christ's ambassadors to love people back to Jesus. We are messengers of good news. Jesus died that we might have true, infinite life in abundance.

We sometimes forget that the word gospel simply means good news. It is easy to get drawn into thinking that the Gospel is some complex, theological structure. But quite the opposite is true! It is so simple that we have worked hard to complicate it. Because the simplicity of the gospel is so hard to grasp, we have surrounded the simplicity with theological walls of complexity. But this message we have been given to deliver is simple, exciting, and amazing. In our unworthy state as sinners, Christ took our sin and paid our debt. In so doing, He made us righteous, which reconciled us to God. We were bound for death and hell, and He gave us life and heaven. He died so that we might live. We were dead, but He made us alive. He took our dead, rotten souls and made us alive. We are now alive in the love of God. What a glorious message we have!

That message is intended for a lost and dying world. We have the answer to their hopeless, helpless struggle to find life and love. In the seventeenth century, Christian philosopher Blais Pascal wrote, "There is a God-shaped vacuum in the heart of each man which cannot be satisfied by any created thing but only by God the Creator, made know through Jesus Christ." What a joy it is to be commissioned to fill that hole in people's lives. Only the love of Christ can fill that emptiness. We have been commissioned as ambassadors of that love. We must allow the love of Christ to flow through us and share the Good News of what He has done for us. As ambassadors of His love, we must simply bring people back to God.

If we are to be ambassadors of Christ, we must be ambassadors of love. Remember, according to I John 4:8, God is love. If the Church could ever fully grasp that idea, the church would look a lot different than it does today. The world would receive us differently if we truly functioned as ambassadors of love. To truly function as Ambassadors of Love, we must act on Christ's behalf and allow Him to love through us.

Destroy the Works of the Devil

As ambassadors of the kingdom of Love, we must remember that we are residing in hostile territory. The kingdom of Love is at war with the kingdom of darkness that rules this age. In John's gospel, Jesus refers to Satan as the ruler of this world on three separate occasions. In John 10:10, Jesus tells us that as the ruler of this age, Satan rules a destructive kingdom. His sole purpose is to steal, kill, and destroy.

As ambassadors of love, life, and abundance, our message is in direct opposition to Satan's system of destruction. Our message of reconciliation to God's wonderful purpose brings destruction to Satan's kingdom. The enemy's plans for destruction are thwarted by the life of God, which is indwelt with love. In John's first letter to the church, he writes that "the Son of God was manifested, that He might destroy the works of the Devil" (1 John 3:8). As His ambassadors, we continue His purpose by spreading the message of reconciliation.

When we operate in love, we operate as an ambassador of Christ. Love motivated everything Jesus did. Love was the driving force that caused Him to leave His throne above and come to earth. He went to the cross because of His love for humanity. No person or power took His life from Him. He laid it down willingly because of His great love. He went into hell and paid the price for our sins because of love. If we operate in any force other than love, we are operating in our flesh and not abiding in Christ.

Faith operating in love is the only way to destroy the works of the devil. His works of killing, stealing, and destroying are all motivated by his hatred of God and His kingdom. The power of God's love is the only thing that can destroy that work and set the captives free. Satan is the father of lies, promising success and delivering destruction. From the very beginning, he has lied to people to keep them in bondage under his rule. He lied to the first family in Genesis 3. He first told them that they would not die if they ate the fruit. Then, he told them they would be like God if they would eat of the Tree of Knowledge of Good and Evil. But they were already like God, and when they ate that fruit, they did die. Satan's joy is the destruction of God's prized creation—humans. As ambassadors of love, our commission is to stop the destruction and end Satan's joy. We serve the One whose great joy is blessing His people—giving them a future and a hope. We are God's messengers of love, commissioned to be ministers of reconciliation and restoration.

When Paul calls us ambassadors for Christ in 2 Corinthians 5, he makes it clear that as ambassadors we are operating on Christ's behalf. He writes, "Now then, we are ambassadors for Christ, as though God were pleading through us: we implore you on Christ's behalf, be reconciled to God." We find this pleading heart of Christ displayed in Matthew 23. Jesus began by condemning the Pharisees for putting heavy, religious burdens upon the people and shutting up the doors of the kingdom of heaven to the masses. Then in verse 37, He said, "Oh, Jerusalem, Jerusalem, how oft would I have gathered you under My wings as a hen does her chicks."

The Bible doesn't tell us where Jesus was standing when He expressed this sorrow. But in my mind, I see Him standing on the Mount of Olives, looking across at the Temple and the city of Jerusalem. He was expressing sorrow for Jerusalem. This is the same Jerusalem that was about to scream, "Crucify Him!" This great cry of compassion is the Father's heart. It is the same protective love a hen has for her chicks.

There is an old adage in the USA that says, "Mad as an old mother hen." Chickens are not aggressive by nature. But if you endanger a hen's chicks, her love for those chicks will alter her natural disposition. If we are going to minister on Christ's behalf, we must have that same heart of love for the masses around us. Our hearts should break at the destruction the enemy brings into people's lives. In the midst of that empathy, a righteous anger should rise up within us. As ambassadors of love, we should be determined to destroy the destructive activity of Satan. Christ's compassion is what compels us to show His love and bring them to the Way.

As ambassadors of love and ministers of reconciliation, we must reveal the goodness of God to hurting people. Many times, the church talks about how much God loves people and then acts as though He hates them. When a Christian says that God hates homosexuals, they have no scriptural basis for their rant. God hates homosexuality because it is a violation of His design. But He loves the homosexual. He loves the homosexual with the same love with which He loves Billy Graham. God did not say that He loved people as long as they were living righteously. Romans 5:8 is explicit in this matter. "For scarcely for a righteous man will one die; yet perhaps for a good man someone would even dare to die. But God demonstrates His own love toward us, in that while we were still sinners, Christ died for us."

Sin is sin—no matter what label it falls under. There are no big sins and little sins. All sin is a matter of unbelief and must be reconciled. The Scriptures tell us that heaven rejoices when one person is reconciled. I believe the converse is also true. When one person dies without being reconciled to God, heaven mourns. Just this week, I received word that the son of a friend of mine died of an overdose. Over the course of thirty years, my friend had done everything he could to free his son from the addiction. But the addiction was simply too strong for the young man. As I was praying for him, the Lord spoke to me. He revealed that He experiences the same sorrow as my friend every time a person dies without receiving salvation. His desire is that "none should perish but that all should come to repentance" (2 Peter 3:9). The Father takes no delight in the sentencing of those who die without Christ.

He has entrusted us with the responsibility of spreading His love as His ambassadors, in order to set sinners free. Through our actions, we spread His love. We testify to the things He has done for us, and we show love to others by our actions towards

128

them. We love because He loved us and filled us with His love. John was called the beloved apostle or the apostle that Jesus loved. He had a special place among the twelve. From that special place, He was well-equipped to explain what it means to be an ambassador of love.

In His first epistle, he writes,

The one who existed from the beginning is the one we have heard and seen. We saw him with our own eyes and touched him with our own hands. He is Jesus Christ, the Word of life. This one who is life from God was shown to us, and we have seen him. And now we testify and announce to you that he is the one who is eternal life. He was with the Father, and then he was shown to us. We are telling you about what we ourselves have actually seen and heard, so that you may have fellowship with us. And our fellowship is with the Father and with his Son, Jesus Christ"

(1 John 1:1-3).

Love is not taught—it must be caught. No matter how much we talk about love and even teach about love, we will only learn to love by being around those who love. John is telling us that he knows about love because he heard it, saw it, and felt it in Jesus. He experienced love in action. He will go on to say that if we say that we are part of God's kingdom and don't express that love to others, we are deceived.

John is saying that He experienced love first-hand. He saw love manifested. He felt it. He was touched by it. The love of Christ forever changed him. He is telling us that he did not simply hear about the love of God. He experienced it. People are tired of hearing about love. They would like to see it in action. We are ambassadors of a father's heart that loves people unconditionally. People tend to put barriers up and try to confine this boundless, amazing love. But His love knows no bounds.

It is a simple fact of human nature that we tend to become like the people with whom we associate. Paul expresses the negative aspects of this truth in 1 Corinthians 15:33. He writes, "Do not be deceived: "Bad company corrupts good morals" (NASB). If we only associate with self-righteous, arrogant people, we will begin to think like them. This will not be our intent, but that association influences us. We know from personal experience that other people can influence us negatively. We warn our children of this fact. As ambassadors, we are to influence people positively.

But Jesus takes our influence to an even higher level. Jesus tells us that we are to compel people to come into the goodness of God. In Luke 14, Jesus tells the parable of the man who gave a great supper and invited people to come and enjoy the festivities. His servants went out to distribute the invitations. But people did not receive the invitations well. Everyone gave excuses as to why they could not attend.

After receiving that rejection, the man hosting the party decided to invite people who would appreciate the invitation. He told his servant to go out into the city and invite the homeless and the helpless. These people responded readily to the invitation. But the feast prepared was so great that even after inviting everyone, there was still room at the banquet. The servant reported to the host that they had done as he had commanded, and the response had been enormous. But there was still room for more.

Luke 14:24 records the final command of the host. He commands, 'Go out into the highways and hedges, and compel them to come in, that my house may be filled. For I say to you that none of those men who were invited shall taste my supper" (Luke 14:16-24).

The Greek word that is translated "compel" in verse 23 is the Greek word *anankazo*. The meaning of this word goes far beyond simply influencing or inviting. This word carries the idea of constraining. That constraining may be by persuasion or entreaty, but most often expresses the idea of threat or force. Of the various meanings, only persuasion is positive. To compel can very literally mean to take by force.

I am not suggesting that we use physical force to convince people to follow Jesus. We are not to physically threaten people to encourage them to repent. That most often leads to a false confession. Much like confessions given under duress or torture. God wants us to compel people to come to Christ by showing them the undisputable love of God. He wants His love to be demonstrated in our lives to such a degree that it becomes a compelling force. Romans 2:4 tells us that the "goodness of God leads you to repentance."

Our goal is to compel people to come into the goodness of our God through the love they observe in us. We are not just talking about going to heaven. We are to compel them to come into a relationship with the Creator, God. Love is our weapon; it is the strongest force on this earth. It is virtually irresistible. We are to love people in such a way that they cannot refuse God. When we full realize what it means to be an ambassador of love, we will discover that this entire process of making disciples is easier than we thought. It is the love of God expressed in us that compels others to be reconciled to this Love.

If you want to compel them to come in, love them even when they are unlovely. Love them even when they are not loving you. The problem is that we want to love those who love us. Jesus said that makes us no better than the rest of the world. We must love those who do not reciprocate our love or don't respond as lovingly as those who love us. Love breaks the enemy's hold on people. When people are drawn to God by experiencing His love, the love does not fade so easily; it just grows deeper and brighter. When they experience the goodness of God and see how He is working in their life to cause good things to happen to them, they are drawn to change their way of thinking (repentance).

Remember, repentance is not condemnation and sorrow. It is simply a change in thinking that leads to a change in behavior. Our love compels us to lovingly warn them that the path they are on is the wrong path. It is like a person driving along and discovering that a bridge over a large canyon has collapsed. His love compels him to warn oncoming vehicles of the danger. The bridge is out, and if they continue down the road, they will experience destruction. Our love will cause us to do everything within our power to save them.

THE LIFE OF AN AMBASSADOR

Our goal as ambassadors is to live a life that ensures that no one is hindered by our poor choices. We should live with so much love exuding from us that people are drawn to Jesus just by being around us. I once heard it said that we are the pipeline through which the oil of the Holy Spirit flows. We must keep the pipeline free of obstructions so the oil can flow freely. And we must keep the pipeline pure so as not to taint the oil. In his second epistle to the church at Corinth, Paul states, "We try to live in such a way that no one will be hindered from finding the Lord by the way we act, and so no one can find fault with our ministry" (II Cor 6:3, NLT).

We must live a life that draws people to the love of God and never hinders anyone from believing. You can only do this by living a life of love. If you believe people are going to come into the Kingdom because you have a well-oiled presentation, you are sadly mistaken. It is often repeated that people will not care how much you know until they know how much you care. We must live a life of pure love that honestly and sincerely cares for others.

A Life of Service

Understanding that fact, we must continually examine our behavior as ambassadors of love. Because we love God and love others as Christ loves, we never want to cause anyone else to stumble. We love others so deeply that we do not want to be involved in any action that might hinder them from following Christ. Paul addresses this in 1 Corinthians 10:23. He writes, "All things are lawful for me, but not all things are helpful; all things are lawful for me, but not all things edify."

When God made you righteous by placing your sin on Jesus, He did not give you a license to sin. It is not helpful or profitable for you to go your own way and act as if God has forgiven you,

132

anyway. If it is not profitable to build up others and encourage them in their relationship with God, do not partake in it.

Paul went a bit further in explaining this concept in 1 Corinthians 9:19-23. "For though I am free from all men, I have made myself a servant to all, that I might win the more; and to the Jews I became as a Jew, that I might win Jews; to those who are under the law, as under the law, that I might win those who are under the law; to those who are without law, as without law (not being without law toward God, but under law toward Christ), that I might win those who are without law; to the weak I became as weak, that I might win the weak. I have become all things to all men, that I might by all means save some. Now this I do for the gospel's sake, that I may be partaker of it with you."

As ambassadors of our Servant King, we live to serve others. Our life as ambassadors is one of service to others so that they may see the love of God in us. For too long, the church has operated as the condemner of unrighteousness, as opposed to the lover of the unrighteous.

A Life of Patient Endurance

The life of an ambassador is not always easy. Loving the unlovely brings challenges to our patience. Trials and tribulations will come, but He has given us the power to endure all that comes against us. These things are part of the life of an Ambassador for Christ. The challenges come because we are behind enemy lines. If you are determined to love, there will be confrontations to that love. It will not always be easy, smooth living. We do not live by this world's system; therefore, this system hates us. We live outside of the world's standards. Bad things happen because the world system is corrupt.

According to John 12:31 and 16:11, Satan is called "the ruler of this world." So, the world system is ruled by the entity that exists to kill, steal, and destroy. This destructive, negative system hates the fact that you love. In 2 Timothy 2, Paul tells us that we must learn to endure hardships and trials because we are strangers and enemies of this evil realm. As a soldier and an ambassador, we will face battles, but the love of God will overcome. The more entangled we are with this world's thinking, the more pressure we will face. Paul warns of this in 2 Corinthians 6:4-5 when he writes, "But in all things, we commend ourselves as ministers of God: in much patience, in tribulations, in needs, in distresses, in stripes, in imprisonments, in tumults, in labors, in sleeplessness, in fastings."

He is warning us that the life of an ambassador of Christ is not without difficulties. The enemy does not give up his land easily. Paul endured many hardships during his love fight: "Three times I was beaten with rods; once I was stoned; three times I was shipwrecked; a night and a day I have been in the deep; in journeys often, in perils of waters, in perils of robbers, in perils of my own countrymen, in perils of the Gentiles, in perils in the city, in perils in the wilderness, in perils in the sea, in perils among false brethren; in weariness and toil, in sleeplessness often, in hunger and thirst, in fastings often, in cold and nakedness—besides the other things, what comes upon me daily: my deep concern for all the churches" (2 Cor 11:25-28).

But remember, "in all these things we are more than conquerors through Him who loved us" (Rom 8:37) because "all things work together for good to those who love God" (Rom 8:28). Paul in no way implies that he was defeated by these difficulties. In the course of his ambassadorship, he had to endure these difficulties. But he came out of them victorious. We must always keep in mind that we are just going through the difficult times. We are not staying in those situations and conditions.

A friend of mine says that his favorite words in the Bible were the simple words, "It came to pass." He always reminds himself that whatever challenges arise, they came to pass—not to stay. It does not matter how difficult things are at the moment. There is an assurance that it will not last. It may last a while or even a significantly long while, but it will pass. If you know it will not last, you can get through it. We are promised that no challenge will ever come upon us that we cannot escape. Paul wrote, "No test or temptation that comes your way is beyond the course of what others have had to face. All you need to remember is that God will never let you down; He'll never let you be pushed past your limit; He'll always be there to help you come through it" (1 Cor 10:13 MESS). He will never let any challenge come upon you that you cannot win. Someone has said, "If you are in it, you can win it."

We must continually prove our love

Your love is demonstrated through your actions, not just through words. In his first letter to the Church, Peter speaks of the proving of your faith to see if it is genuine. Not only are we challenged to prove our faith, we are also challenged to prove our love. The principle of proving is not a test to see how much we know or how well we behave. Rather, it is proving, as in proving the steel of a sword.

In day gone by, a soldier needed to have confidence in his weapon. So, the swords were "proven" before being brought into use. For instance, the British army used a 6-point proof of their swords. The sword was proven to maintain its edge after striking a hard object. Five other tests were used to prove that the sword would remain straight even when severely flexed. The proving assured the soldiers that their weapons were of the highest quality.

The challenges to the Ambassadors love are there to assure the ambassador that "no weapon formed against him would prosper" (Isaiah 54:17) and "that neither death nor life, nor angels nor principalities nor powers, nor things present nor things to come, nor height nor depth, nor any other created thing, shall be able to separate us from the love of God which is in Christ Jesus our Lord" (Rom 8:38-39).

Our endurance of these trials and tribulations also proves our ambassadorship to others. 2 Corinthians 6:4,6 explains this proving. "In everything we do, we show that we are true ministers of God. We patiently endure troubles and hardships and calamities of every kind . . .We prove ourselves by our purity, our understanding, our patience, our kindness, by the Holy

Spirit within us, and by our sincere love" (NLT). By our life, we prove our ambassadorship. People see our purity and compassionate, loving understanding. They are touched by our patience and kindness. But most importantly they know us by our love.

A Purposeful Life

Each of us has a main purpose in life – that we might help reconcile people to God. We are on a mission from God to spread His love to those around us and compel them to come to Him. Christ commissioned us as His ambassadors. Paul expressed his ambassadorship this way: "I endure all things for the elect's sake, that they, too, may be saved" (2 Tim 2:10). As an ambassador for Christ, you will endure some unpleasantries.

Everyone you love is not going to reciprocate your love. But you must love without limitation or restriction. Your love must be an enduring love. If it is an enduring love, it will be a love that gives until the end. Love that cannot endure will never satisfy. It will never touch others with love. It is that love that lasts that touches us. Anyone can say, "I love you." It is easy to love someone for a day. It is much harder to love day after day–to love through the faults and failures, to love through the betrayal and heartache.

We can talk about Jesus and the Gospel for hours. We can share great truths and teachings. But the thing that people remember will be the love that we show. We are called to be God's ambassadors on this earth. Our sole responsibility is to spread the love of God with our actions. We must show the world this Good News that we have found. The sheer joy of love inside of us because of what Jesus did . . . as well as the love He has given us. . . will draw people to the Way. It is then that His love can fully break the bondages in their lives and place them in a relationship with the Creator of all.

It is then that we fulfill our commission as
Ambassadors of Love.

136

The Essentials of the Faith series is now available in twenty-seven languages. For information about copies your language, please contact us at the addresses below.. Books 1 -3 can also be purchased on Amazon Kindle. All proceeds from the sale of these books goes directly into missions.

USA
CITIPOINTE CHURCH
307 N First St
Wylie, Texas 75098 USA
972.442.9111

mailbox@citipointe.org
pastor@citipointe.org

www.ingramcontent.com/pod-product-compliance
Lightning Source LLC
LaVergne TN
LVHW051558080426
835510LV00020B/3029